# KENTUCKY'S LITERARY LANDSCAPE

## The Kentucky Writers Hall of Fame (2013-2017)

# KENTUCKY'S LITERARY LANDSCAPE

## The Kentucky Writers
## Hall of Fame (2013-2017)

*James B. Goode*

JESSE STUART
FOUNDATION
Ashland, Kentucky
2017

ISBN: 978-1-938471-62-9

Published by
Jesse Stuart Foundation
4440 13th Street
Ashland, Kentucky 41102
(606) 326-1667
jsfbooks.com

# DEDICATION

*For all those Kentucky writers who have made this Commonwealth the literary capital of Mid-America.*

## SPECIAL THANKS TO:

*• Amy Morgan for her friendship and astute editing*

*• Susanna Hart Lawrence, my loving partner, for all her support during this process*

*• Photographers and publishing houses who provided valuable resources*

*• Members of the Kentucky Writers Hall of Fame Committee*

**EDITOR'S NOTE:**

In order to make the bibliographic information more accessible, electronic source citations have been formatted in a modified MLA style.

# TABLE OF CONTENTS

# Preface

In February 2017, Barbara Kingsolver stood beside a poster-sized photo of herself as she addressed an audience of 350 assembled at the Carnegie Center in Lexington, Kentucky. She had just been inducted into the Kentucky Writers Hall of Fame, and she admitted it was both a thrill and a challenge. "That is a job to live up to the name Kentucky writer," she said. "I think about it all the time. I don't take it for granted."

Neither should the rest of us. While Kentucky has long been branded as a state with limited literacy, it has at the same time produced some of the nation's greatest writers. The first African-American novelist was born (a slave) near Lexington. The nation's first million-selling author came from Bourbon County, Ky. The country's first poet laureate was Robert Penn Warren, of Guthrie, Ky., who won three Pulitzer Prizes.

In more recent times, Poet Nikky Finney, a University of Kentucky English professor, won the 2011 National Book Award. A year later, Wendell Berry of Henry County won the federal government's top literary honor, the National Humanities Medal. Meanwhile, Sue Grafton of Louisville has just kept spinning out alphabet-based thrillers; *Z is for Zero,* her last in a 26-book series, is scheduled for release in 2019.

The idea for the Kentucky Writers Hall of Fame arose at the Carnegie Center in 2010. Staff and board members had become aware of both the 200-year legacy of great Kentucky writing and a recent spate of well-published authors in the state. They decided it was time to honor the commonwealth's best authors, hoping also to inspire young writers to develop their craft.

For its first two years, 2013 and 2014, the Hall of Fame inducted only deceased authors. Early inductees included Robert Penn Warren (*All the King's Men*), Harriette Arnow (*The Doll-maker*), Harry Caudill (*Night Comes to the Cumberlands*, and William Wells Brown (*Clotel, the President's Daughter*). That set the literary foundation for the Hall.

In the Hall of Fame's third year, 2015, the first living writer was inducted: Wendell Berry. In his remarks that night, Berry spoke about an urgent role for writers. "Much that we have now that is of greatest value has come to us from books," he reminded the audience. "Our Constitution and Bill of Rights—just to hint at an immeasurable abundance—have come to us from books and from readers of books. To keep our heritage viable and transmissible will require capable writers of books, capable readers of books, and a capable culture of literacy, however small it may have to be."

A year later, in accepting her induction into the Hall of Fame, Bobbie Ann Mason of Mayfield tried to explain why Kentuckians produce so much outstanding literature. "A rich heritage of writers occurs when creative people meet an abundance of irresistible or urgent story material," she said. "We can't help it. Somebody's gotta do it. Writers and artists have to interpret what is important, what is going on in the world and in our hearts."

It wasn't the first time someone tried to identify the

Kentucky writing mystique. More than a decade earlier, University of Kentucky professor James Baker Hall wrote an article titled, "How Come There Are So Many Good Writers in Kentucky?" He mused: "Is it explained simply by the existence of limestone in the drinking water, or is it more complex than that? Does our proximity to the big caves work us in our sleep, leading us to dig deeper and stay under longer, to comprehend more readily that the rocking world rests on the back of a turtle emerging from slumber?"

I am not sure whether turtles are part of the answer. But undoubtedly, the natural beauty of Kentucky has played a role in producing poets and novelists. Kentucky writers often set their work among the commonwealth's undulating hills, dangerous rock formations, running rivers and waterfalls. And the plots are thick with conflict—reflecting the long and lingering Kentucky battles: urban vs. rural, North vs. South, Hatfield vs. McCoy.

The Carnegie Center is excited that in just five years, the Kentucky Writers Hall of Fame has become a high point each year for the state's writing community—and that it has become the subject of this book. The Carnegie Center echoes the hopes of Ms. Mason, who said in her 2016 Hall of Fame induction speech: "Kentucky has been fortunate. In Kentucky, we are brimming over with creative writers. Students all over the state can meet poets and novelists. Students can discover worlds beyond themselves and in themselves. They can imagine that they can be heroes." Just like the 29 writers in this book.

Neil Chethik, Director
Carnegie Center/Kentucky Writers Hall of Fame
Lexington, Kentucky

# Introduction

Kentucky's rich literary history spans well over 200 years, beginning with travelers who passed through the Commonwealth exploring the territory west of the Allegany Mountains and who wrote of their experiences in this new and mysterious land.

Literary historian John Wilson Townsend, in his landmark work, *Kentucky in American Letters* (1913), mentions a litany of writers who explored the early literary landscape.

Notable among these are: French botanist Francois Andre Michaux's *Travels to the West of the Alleghany Mountains, in the States of Ohio, Kentucky, and Tennessee* (1805), Breton explorer Fortescue Cuming's *Tour to the Western Country, Through Ohio and Kentucky* (1807), and Scottish botanist John Bradbury's *Travels in the Interior of America* (1817).

Townsend's *Kentucky in American Letters 1784-1912*, published in two volumes, is one of the earliest works to take a comprehensive look at Kentucky's writers from the 18th through the early 20th Century. In his introduction, Townsend says he identified 1,000 Kentucky writers but could only feature 196 in volumes I & II.

Volume I highlighted such luminaries as: John Uri Lloyd,

Henry Watterson, Henry Clay, Stephen C. Foster, John J. Audubon, Jefferson Davis, William O. Butler, Zachary Taylor, John Filson, and Theodore O'Hara. Among the ninety authors featured in Volume II, are notables: Joseph Seamon Cotter, Sr., Annie Fellows Johnson, John Fox, Jr., Madison Cawein, Alice Hegan Rice, Lucy Furman, Irvin S. Cobb, and James Lane Allen.

Sixty-three years later, Dorothy Townsend finished her husband's work on a third volume by including 119 writers in *Kentucky in American Letters Volume Three* (1976). Among those presented in Volume III are: Harriette Simpson Arnow, Wendell Berry, Harry M. Caudill, Rebecca Caudill, Thomas D. Clark, Janis Holt Giles, A. B. Guthrie, Jr., Gayl Jones, Jim Wayne Miller, John Jacob Niles, Jean Ritchie, James Still, Jesse Stuart, Allen Tate, Walter Tevis, and Robert Penn Warren.

Another significant book is William S. Ward's *Literary History of Kentucky* (1988) which divides the history
of Kentucky literature into three periods: 1) Before 1860 2) Coming of Age 1860-1930, and 3) Maturity 1930-1980. Famed Kentucky historian Thomas D. Clark says in his introduction:

> *Almost unanimously Kentucky's authors have in some way fallen under the spell of the land and its penetrating environmental influence in molding personality and setting the course of the state's history. If there is such a thing as a composite Kentucky personality, spirit, or sentimentality, it is firmly fixed in the deeply grooved agrarian-rural traditions which have rigidly bonded people in their responses to the subtleties and recurrences of place and land.*

At the advent of the 20th century and following into the 21st, Kentucky writers did not abandon agrarian themes but moved to explore emerging environmental, political, religious, biological, sociological, and economic concerns.

Literary historian Ish Richey's *Kentucky Literature 1784-1963* (1963) is a useful tool for exploring 114 of Kentucky's most prominent imaginative writers during this period. Fifteen of the featured writers are Kentucky Writers Hall of Fame (KWHOF) inductees. Ritchey's work includes short biographical sketches, brief bibliographic information, and writing excerpts. He also includes a bibliographic addendum of criticism, biographies, bibliographies, and unpublished theses and dissertations.

Five years later, Sister Mary Carmel Browning published *Kentucky Authors: A History of Kentucky Literature* (1968). What began with a college class survey of Kentucky poets grew into an eight-chapter book that includes the sixty-two writers featuring historians, journalists, poets, novelists, dramatists, children's writers, regional writers, learned advisers in the field of Kentucky literature, and collections of Kentuckiana. This work also contains an introduction by Thomas D. Clark and a partial bibliography for each writer.

Literary scholar Joy Pennington's *Selected Kentucky Literature* (1980) features eleven short fiction writers, eleven poets, and three dramatists. This volume includes what may be the only poem published by Harriette Arnow: "Ode to a Purple Aluminum Christmas Tree."

Pennington reminds us of the quality of Kentucky writers in her introduction:

*Many [Kentucky writers] have transcended the region to be recognized nationally and internation-*

*ally. Rebecca Caudill, Harriette Simpson Arnow, James Still, Hollis Summers, Jesse Stuart, and Allen Tate have received numerous literary awards. A.B. Guthrie, Jr. and Robert Penn Warren have won Pulitzer Prizes; in fact, Robert Penn Warren has won the Pulitzer in two different genres, once in fiction and twice in poetry.*

Wade Hall's *The Kentucky Anthology: Two Hundred Years in the Bluegrass State* (2005), published ninety-two years after Townsend's first two volumes, features seventy-nine authors and 254 works. Hall says in his introduction, "In the early years, they are hunters, soldiers, and adventurers, travelers and tourists, land speculators and Indian fighters, even outlaws; later, they are farmers, lawyers, preachers, physicians, and educators; and more recently they are journalists, historians, playwrights, novelists, and poets."

Four other anthologies of note are: Hollis Summers' *Kentucky Story* (1954), a short story collection featuring fifteen prominent Kentucky writers; Morris Grubbs' short story anthology *Home and Beyond* (2001) featuring forty-two writers; George Ella Lyon's *A Kentucky Christmas* (2003) spotlighting seventy-three authors of essays, poems, and short fiction; and James B. Goode's *Kentucky's Twelve Days of Christmas* (2012), including poems, songs, novel excerpts, short fiction, creative non-fiction, and memoir excerpts from thirty-four writers with Kentucky connections.

There has long been a debate about the criteria for including an author in the canon of Kentucky literature. Many anthologists, including Richey and Pennington, define a Kentucky author as a writer born in Kentucky or one who has resided there. In his introduction to *Kentucky in American Letters*, Townsend describes his criteria for including a writer for his anthologies: "I have regarded the birthplace of a piece of literature more important than that of the author."

Essentially, both the birther/resident proponents and Townsend's definition have been integral guiding principles in the selection criteria used by the Kentucky Writers Hall of Fame Committee. Of the twenty-nine writers inducted into the Kentucky Writers Hall of Fame from 2012-2017, nine were born outside Kentucky. All but three of those are Southern writers, with many of their works set in Kentucky or with Kentucky at their core. Of the twenty born in the state, nine are from Central Kentucky, seven from Eastern Kentucky, one from Northern Kentucky, and three from Western Kentucky.

This volume is a celebration of the first five years of the Kentucky Writers Hall of Fame and the twenty-nine writers, who have been inducted into this prestigious Hall. There dozens more who deserve the honor and the Hall of Fame Selection Committee looks forward to continuing this tradition.

James B. Goode, Coordinator
Carnegie Center/Kentucky Writers Hall of Fame
Professor Emeritus, BCTC
Lexington, Kentucky

# CHAPTER ONE
## 2013

# Harriette Simpson Arnow
## 1908-1986

Wayne County, Kentucky native Harriette Louisa Simpson Arnow is best known for her landmark novel *The Dollmaker* (1954) that chronicled the outmigration of rural Appalachians to the industrial centers of America at the advent of World War II. *The Dollmaker* was widely read, remaining on best-seller lists for over 32 weeks. This work became one of the most famous Appalachian novels of the 20th century and is currently still in print. This novel was actually meant to be the final novel in a trilogy that included *Mountain Path* (1936) and *Hunter's Horn* (1949). She also authored a novel *Between the Flowers* in 1938, that went unpublished until 1999. Her other notable books included: two historical works, *Seedtime on the Cumberland* (1960) and *Flowering of the Cumberland* (1963), two additional novels, *The Weedkiller's Daughter* (1970) and *The Kentucky Trace* (1974), one biographical work, *Old Burnside* (1976), and a collection of short fiction, *The Collected Short Stories of Harriette Simpson Arnow* (2005).

*Hunter's Horn* won the 1949 *Saturday Review* Best Novel Award, beating George Orwell's classic, *1984*. This novel was picked by the *New York Times Book Review* as one of the top ten novels of that year. The *Dollmaker* was runner up to William Faulkner's, *A Fable*, for the 1955 National Book Award and finished runner-up in the final voting for the Pulitzer Prize in Fiction the same year, close behind Faulkner's *A Fable*. Arnow finished ahead of Randall Jarrell *Pictures from an Institution* and John Steinbeck's *Sweet Thursday*. Actress Jane Fonda starred in the 1984 film adaptation made-for-television movie version of *The Dollmaker*. For this performance, Fonda received a Prime-time Emmy Award for outstanding Lead Actress—Miniseries or Movie.

Joyce Carol Oates wrote in *The New York Times Book Review* that Arnow's *The Dollmaker* is ". . . our most unpretentious American masterpiece." Because of the Detroit scenes in the novel, this work has been compared to earlier writers such as Rebecca Harding Davis, Upton Sinclair, and Tillie Olsen, whose writing was rooted in chronicling the plight of the urban industrial worker.

Numerous critics have pointed out that Arnow's portrait of Gertie, a woman of great physical and psychological strength, reached the American public at a time when strong images of women were rare. An example of Arnow's own struggle was her foiled attempt to be published in *Esquire*. Out of frustration over attempts to get published as a female writer, she assumed a male pseudonym and submitted a story under the moniker H. L. Simpson, along with a photograph of her brother-in-law. The story was accepted and appeared in the July 1942 issue.

Arnow was educated at Burnside High School, Berea College, and the University of Louisville. After teaching in a Louisville school for a few months, Simpson fell ill. She retreated to a resort in northern Michigan, where she wrote her first novel, *Mountain Path* (1936). From 1934-1939, she lived in Cincinnati and worked for the Federal Writer's Project of the WPA. There she met her future husband Harold B. Arnow, a Chicago news-paperman. They married in 1939 and moved to the Kentucky hills of Pulaski County near Burnside, where she taught school for a brief time. In 1944, they moved to Detroit where jobs were readily available during World War II. They had two children—Marcella Jane and Thomas Louis.

Arnow died March 22, 1986 on her farm in Washtenaw County, Michigan and is buried in the William Casada Cemetery in Pulaski County, Kentucky.

### Sources

Ballard, Sandra. "Harriette Simpson Arnow: A Biographical Sketch." *Appalachian Heritage*. 40:2. Spring 2012. 24-25. Print.

Eckley, Wilton. "Harriette Louise (Simpson) Arnow." *The Kentucky Encyclopedia*. Ed. John Kelber. Lexington, KY.: U P of Kentucky, 1992. 32. Print.

"Essay on The Dollmaker by Harriette Arnow." Online. Accessed 27 Jul. 2014. <http://www.essayempire.com/customessay/lit-erature-research-paper-topics/american-literature/3672.html>.

Chung, Haeja K., ed. *Harriette Simpson Arnow: critical essays on her work*. East Lansing, MI: Michigan State U P, 1995. *Project MUSE*. Online. Accessed 27 Jul. 2014. <http://muse.jhu.edu/>.

"Harriette Simpson Arnow." *Kentucky in American Letters: Volume III 1913-1975*. Ed. Dorothy Edwards Townsend. Georgetown, KY: Georgetown College P, 1976. Print. 18-19.

"Harriette Simpson Arnow." The University of Louisville A&S Hall of Honor. Online. Accessed 23 Jul. 2014. <https://louisville.edu/artsandsciences/about/hallofhonor/inductees/arnow.html>.

## Selected Bibliography

### Biographical

*Old Burnside*. Lexington, KY: U P of Kentucky, 1976. Print.

### History

*Seedtime on the Cumberland*. New York: The Macmillan Company, 1960. Print.

*Flowering of the Cumberland*. New York: The Macmillan Company, 1963. Print.

### Novels

*Mountain Path*. New York: Convici Friede, 1936. Print.

*Hunter's Horn*. New York: Macmillan, 1949. Print.

*The Dollmaker*. New York: The Macmillan Company, 1954. Print.

*The Weedkiller's Daughter*. New York: Alfred A. Knopf, 1970. Print.

*The Kentucky Trace*. New York: Alfred A. Knopf, 1974. Print.

*Between the Flowers*. East Lansing: Michigan State UP, 1999.

### Short Fiction

*The Collected Short Stories of Harriette Simpson Arnow*. Ed. Sandra Ballard and Haeja K. Chung. East Lansing: Michigan State UP, 2005.

# William Wells Brown

## 1814-1884

Playwright, journalist, novelist, and historian William Wells Brown's popular autobiography, *Narrative of William H. Brown, a Fugitive Slave, Written by Himself*, was published in 1847, but had been preempted by Frederick Douglass' *Narrative of the Life of Frederick Douglass, an American Slave* in 1845 and did not ultimately achieve the fame of his predecessor. Both writers were skilled public speakers and traveled widely to promote their work; yet Brown eventually slipped into relative obscurity. He is said to have feuded with Douglas for most of his life.

Eza Greenspan, Brown's biographer and author of *William Wells Brown: An African-American Life*, has said that "As a student of the public record, whether engraved on public memorials or recorded in state archives, he so frequently encountered the pattern of deliberate or casual omission that he developed a term for it— colonization." Greenspan has not been able to solve the mystery of why Douglas remains a major symbol of his time, while Brown does not. But his 600-page biography goes a long way toward helping Brown regain his rightful place in American letters.

Although Brown says in his narrative that he was born in Lexington, Kentucky, he was actually born on a Montgomery County farm near Mount Sterling. His mother was a slave and his father, James W. Higgins, was the slave owner's cousin. He was brought, at age 3, to Marthasville in Warren County near St. Louis, Missouri.

At age nineteen, after sixteen years of enslavement, he escaped in 1834 to free territory in Ohio. He made a concentrated effort to educate himself after almost two decades of illiteracy. Brown became a conductor on the Underground Railroad and worked on a Lake Erie steamer ferrying slaves to freedom in Canada. In 1843, Brown became a lecturing agent for the New York Anti-Slavery Society and worked closely with William Lloyd Garrison and Wendell Phillips.

He then moved to England and became a celebrity as an anti-slavery crusader, before returning to the United States in 1854 as a man of letters. Brown became freed slave upon his return to the United States, because supporters in England purchased his freedom. He settled in Boston, Massachusetts.

He published a travelogue *Three Years in Europe* (1852) followed by his now famous sensational novel *Clotel; or, The President's Daughter* (1853). This was the first novel to be published in the United States by an African-American. The title character is the daughter of a slave fathered by President Thomas Jefferson. The book's inspiration arose from persistent rumors about Jefferson's now-proven relationship with his mixed-race slave, Sally Hemmings, who bore several of his children.

In 1863, he published a groundbreaking history of African-Americans *The Black Man*. In 1867, he followed with a history of African-American involvement in the Civil War *The Negro in the American Rebellion*. His final book was *My Southern Home* (1880), which Greenspan calls a "savagely perceptive, rollicking account of the South looking both backward and forward from a Jim Crow-era vantage point." He is also the first published black playwright. He reportedly often read his play, "The Escape; or, A Leap for Freedom" (1858), at abolitionists rallies.

He died November 6, 1884 in Chelsea, Massachusetts. He is buried in an unmarked grave in the Cambridge, Massachusetts Cemetery.

## Sources

Eblen, Tom. "Black History Month: Scholar's Research on Author William Wells Brown Finds New Truths About His Life." *Kentucky.com Lexington Herald Leader*. 19 Feb. 2013. Online. <http://www.kentucky.com/2013/02/19/2522414/tom-eblen-black-history-month.html#storylink=cpy>.

Farrison, William Edward. "William Wells Brown." *The Kentucky Encyclopedia*. Ed. John Kleber. Lexington, KY.: U P of Kentucky, 1992. 131-132. Print.

Greenspan, Ezra. *William Wells Brown: An African-American Life*. New York: W. W. Norton, 2014. Print.

Weinberg, Steve. "Author William Wells Brown, a former slave, comes out of obscurity in new biography." *Books: The Kansas City Star*. 24 July 2014. Online. Accessed 30 Jul. 2014. <http://www.kansascity.com/entertainment/books/article78327 3.html>.

"William Wells Brown." Spartacus Educational. Online. Accessed 30 Jul. 2014. <http://spartacus-educational.com/com/ USAbrownW.htm>.

*William Wells Brown: A Reader*. Ed. Ezra Greenspan. Athens, GA: U of Georgia P, 2008. Print.

### Selected Bibliography

*Narrative of William W. Brown, a Fugitive Slave. Written by Himself*. Boston: The Anti-slavery office, 1847. Print.

*The Anti-Slavery Harp: A Collection of Songs for Anti-Slavery Meetings*. Boston: Bela Marsh, 1848. Print.

*Narrative of William W. Brown, an American Slave. Written by Himself*. London: C. Gilpin, 1849. Print.

*Three Years in Europe: Or, Places I Have Seen and People I Have Met*. London: Charles Gilpin, 1852. Print.

*Clotel; or the President's Daughter*. London, UK: Partridge & Oakley, 1853. Print.

*The American Fugitive in Europe. Sketches of Places and People Abroad*. Boston: John P. Jewett, 1855. Print.

*The Black Man: His Antecedents, His Genius, and His Achievements*. New York: Thomas Hamilton; Boston: R.F. Wallcut, 1863. Print.

*The Negro in the American Rebellion; His Heroism and His Fidelity...* Boston: Lee & Shepard, 1867. Print.

*The Rising Son, or The Antecedents and Advancements of the Colored Race*. Boston: A. G. Brown & Co., 1873. Print.

*My Southern Home: or, The South and Its People*. Boston: A. G. Brown & Co., Publishers, 1880. Print.

# Harry Caudill

## 1922-1990

Historian, novelist, essayist, and columnist Harry M. Caudill's seminal work *Night Comes to the Cumberlands: A Biography of a Depressed Area* was published in 1963. This book caught the attention of the highest levels of leadership in the United States and significantly contributed to the emergence of the War on Poverty during the Kennedy/Johnson administrations. President John F. Kennedy appointed a commission to investigate conditions in the region and his successor, Lyndon B. Johnson, made Appalachia a keystone in his War on Poverty movement.

Caudill, a native of Letcher County, Kentucky, grew up in

27

the coalfields of Eastern Kentucky. He served in Italy during World War II and suffered a debilitating injury from which he struggled the rest of his life. After returning from the War, he enrolled in The University of Kentucky Law School, met and married Anne Fry in 1946, before graduating and returning to his beloved Letcher County; where he established a law practice which lasted over 28 years. In addition to his work as a barrister, he was a politician who served as President of the Letcher County Bar Association and three two-year terms as a State Representative in the Kentucky State Legislature (1953, 1955, & 1959).

Caudill published ten books, over eighty newspaper essays, fifty magazine articles, and penned more than 120 speeches and lectures. Most were focused on the social, economic, and environmental issues of Appalachia. Critics called him "the Upton Sinclair of the coal fields." He was active with the Sierra Club, The Audubon Society, and local advocacy groups such as the Pike County Citizens Association, and the Appalachian Group to Save the Land and People. The University of Kentucky awarded him an Honorary Doctorate of Laws in 1971. He won the Appalachian Studies Association Weatherford Award in 1976.

Experiencing increasing pain from the leg injury he suffered in WWII and facing the prolonged effects of Parkinson's disease, Caudill took his own life on the afternoon of November 29, 1990. He is buried in the Battle Grove Cemetery in Cynthiana, Kentucky.

Glenn Fowler of *The New York Times* wrote in his obituary: *[Caudill was] a strenuous orator who liked to quote in a sonorous mountain drawl from the Bible, Shakespeare, Tennyson and Dickens, he was principally concerned with improving public education, conserving land and resources and reforming the judiciary. He co-sponsored a 1954 law that set minimum support levels for public schools and imposed a sales tax to pay the cost.*

## Sources

"Biography/History." Anne and Harry M. Caudill Collection, 1854-1996, 91M2, Special Collections and Digital Programs, University of Kentucky Libraries, Lexington. Online. Accessed 7 Aug. 2014.
<http://kdl.kyvl.org/catalog/xt79gh9b5x4t/guide>.

Brosi, George. "Harry M. Caudill: An Annotated Bibliography." *Appalachian Heritage* 21.2 (1993): 47-48. *Project MUSE.* Online. Accessed 7 Aug. 2014.
<https://muse.jhu.edu/login?auth=0&type=summary&url=/journals/appalachian_heritage/v021/21.2.brosi.pdf>.

Fowler, Glenn. "Harry M. Caudill, 68, Who Told of Appalachian Poverty." *nytimes.com* 1 December 2009. Online. Accessed 7 Aug. 2014.
<http://www.nytimes.com/1990/12/01/obituaries/harry-m-caudill-68-who-told-of-appalachian-poverty.html>.

"The Harry Caudill Collection." *Berea College Hutchins Library Archives and Special Collections.* Online. Accessed 7 Aug. 2014.
<http://community.berea.edu/hutchinslibrary/specialcollec-tions/saa74.asp>.

"Harry Caudill." *Kentucky in American Letters: Volume III 1913-1975.* Ed. Dorothy Edwards Townsend. Georgetown, KY: Georgetown College P, 1976. 48-51. Print.

Mueller, Lee. "Harry Monroe Caudill." *The Kentucky Encyclopedia.* Ed. John Kelber. Lexington, KY: U P of Kentucky, 1992. 172-173. Print.

## Selected Bibliography

### Anecdotes & Tales

*The Mountain, the Miner, and the Lord and Other Tales from a Country Law Office.* Lexington, KY: U P of Kentucky, 1980. Print.

*Slender is the Thread: Tales from a Country Law Office.* Lexington, KY: U P of Kentucky, 1987. Print.

### Essays

*Caudill, Harry, Eliot Porter, and Edward Abbey. Appalachian Wilderness: The Great Smoky Mountains.* New York: Dutton, 1970. Print.

*Lester's Progress.* Kentucke Imprints: Berea, KY, 1986. Print.

### History/Social Criticism

*Night Comes to the Cumberlands: A Biography of a Depressed Area.* Boston: Little, Brown and Co., 1963. Print.

*My Land Is Dying.* New York: E.P. Dutton, 1971. Print.

*The Watches of the Night.* Boston: Little, Brown and Co., 1976. Print.

*A Darkness at Dawn: Appalachian Kentucky and the Future.* Lexington, KY: U P of Kentucky, 1976. Print.

*Theirs Be the Power: The Moguls of Eastern Kentucky.* Urbana, IL: University of Illinois P, 1983. Print.

### Novels

*Dark Hills to Westward: The Saga of Jenny Wiley.* Boston: Atlantic, Little-Brown, 1969.

_____ (reprint). Ashland, KY: Jesse Stuart Foundation, 1994. Print.

*The Senator from Slaughter County.* Boston: Atlantic, Little-Brown, 1973. Print.

_____ (reprint). Ashland, KY: Jesse Stuart Foundation, 1997. Print.

# Elizabeth Madox Roberts

## 1881-1941

Perryville, Kentucky native Elizabeth Madox Roberts' best known novels— *The Time of Man* (1926) and *The Great Meadow* (1930) were both short-listed for the Pulitzer Prize in Fiction. During her short life of 60 years, she published seven novels, three volumes of poems, and two collections of short stories. Her work received critical acclaim from Carl and Mark Van Doren, Robert Penn Warren, Ford Madox Ford, Sherwood Anderson, Sylvia Townsend Warner, and other prominent writers and critics of her time.

Initially, she was criticized as mystical and obscure, but having a superb rhythmic style that was effused with the power of suggestion. She had great instinct for Kentucky folk speech, and was an expert in capturing descriptions of Kentucky folk culture. One critic described her as "... a writer of authentic regional power with an international reputation."

Her family moved to Springfield, Kentucky where she attended Washington County public schools, but then Roberts moved to Covington, Kentucky to live with her maternal grandparents and attend high school. In 1900, she enrolled at the University of Kentucky (then the State College of Kentucky), but stayed only one semester. She dropped out due to a serious health condition, moved back to Springfield, and taught school for ten years. She left Springfield in 1910 and moved to Colorado to live with her sister.

At the suggestion of a professor friend, she enrolled at the University of Chicago in 1917 at age 36. The University fostered an active literary community, which led her to form life-long friendships with a group of writers and artists who were members of the Chicago Poetry Club, including: Glenway Wescott, Janet Lewis, Yvor Winters, Monroe Wheeler, and Maurice Lesemann.

She graduated Phi Beta Kappa with a B.A. in English in 1921. In 1922, she was awarded the Fiske Prize for a group of poems printed in a privately published book of poetry *Under the Tree*.

Roberts won numerous awards for her writing including: The John Reed Memorial Prize in 1928, The O. Henry Memorial Short Story Prize in 1930, and The Poetry Society of South Carolina's Prize in 1931.

Because of her diagnosis of terminal Hodgkin's disease in 1936, she began wintering in Florida near Orlando. She returned to Springfield for the summers to be with her parents. She died in Orlando in 1941. Her remains were returned to Springfield, Kentucky for burial at Cemetery Hill.

## Sources

"Biography of Elizabeth Maddox Roberts." PoemHunter.com. Online.
Accessed 1 Aug. 2014.
<http://www.poemhunter.com/elizabeth-madox-roberts/
biography/>.

"Elizabeth Madox Roberts." *Kentucky in American Letters: Volume
III 1913-1975*. Ed. Dorothy Edwards Townsend. Georgetown,
KY: Georgetown College P, 1976. 276-280. Print.

The Elizabeth Maddox Roberts Society: Literary Works. Online.
Accessed 1 Aug. 2014. <http://emrsociety.com/>.

"Guide to the Maurice Lesemann Papers 1918-1986: Biographical
Note on Elizabeth Maddox Roberts." *Stanford University
Library: Department of Special Collections: Online Archives of
California*. Online. Accessed 1 Aug. 2014.
<http://cdn.calisphere.org/data/13030/43/tf1j49n543/files/tf1j4
9n543.pdf>.

## Selected Bibliography

### Novels

*The Time of Man*. New York: Viking Press, 1926. Print.
*My Heart and My Flesh*. New York: Viking Press, 1927. Print.
*Jingling in the Wind*. New York: Viking Press, 1928. Print.
*The Great Meadow*. New York: Viking Press, 1930. Print.
*A Buried Treasure*. New York: Viking Press, 1931. Print.
*He Sent Forth a Raven*. New York: Viking Press, 1935. Print.
*Black Is My True Love's Hair*. New York: Viking, 1938. Print.
*Song in the Meadow*. New York: Viking Press, 1940. Print.

### Poetry

*In the Great Steep's Garden*. Colorado: Privately Published, 1915.
Print.
*Under the Tree*. New York: B. W. Huebsch, 1922. Print.

### Short Fiction

*The Haunted Mirror*. New York: Viking Press, 1932. Print.
*Not by Strange Gods*. New York: Viking Press, 1941. Print.

Photograph by Dean Cadle/Courtesy University Press of Kentucky.

# James Still

## 1906-2001

Poet, novelist, short story writer, and folklorist James Still says in his autobiography, "I appeared in this world July 16, 1906, on Double Branch Farm near La Fayette in Chambers County, Alabama.

Still worked his way through Lincoln Memorial University in Harrogate, Tennessee where he graduated in 1921. His class-mates included Jesse Stuart, who also became one of the most widely published writers from Kentucky. He began graduate school at Vanderbilt University in 1929, earning his M.A. in English in 1930. He also attended University of Illinois and received a Bachelor of Science in Library Science.

While Still was at Vanderbilt, members of the now famous Fugitives were on the verge of publishing their *I'll Take My Stand* (1930), a manifesto on Jeffersonian agrarianism. Still was educated by such luminaries as: Edwin Mims, Robert Penn Warren, John Crowe Ransom, Andrew Lytle, John Donald Wade, and Clyde Curry (who directed his thesis "The Function of Dreams and Visions in the Middle English Romances").

Still came to Hindman, Kentucky in 1931 with one of his Vanderbilt classmates, poet and social activist Don West, to work with students for the summer. Just as the summer ended, the librarian at Hindman Settlement School resigned. Still gladly accepted the position and, except for a stint as a soldier during World War II in Africa and the Middle East from 1942-1944, he spent the next 70 years in Hindman.

Still penned his masterpiece novel *River of Earth* in a rented two-story log cabin on the Dead Mare Branch of Little Carr Creek in Knott County, Kentucky (once occupied by famed Appalachian Dulcimer maker, Jethro Amburgey). The landmark novel was released February 5, 1940. In this novel, Still expertly reveals the dilemma prompted by changes coming to Appalachia during the emergence of the coal industry. This fictional depiction portrays the struggles of a rural agrarian mountain family eking out their living through the tradition of subsistence farming, as opposed to the encroaching culture of the coal mines in eastern Kentucky and those succumbing to the lure of an hourly wage job. Still received the Southern Author's Award shortly after publication, and shared the award with Thomas Wolfe for his novel *You Can't Go Home Again*.

Still published fourteen books including three volumes of poetry, three novels, four short story collections, two books on

Appalachian folklife, and two children's picture books. His stories and poems appeared in numerous magazines including: *The Atlantic, The Yale Review, Saturday Review, The Saturday Evening Post, Esquire, The Virginia Quarterly Review,* as well as in textbooks and anthologies.

Several of Still's short stories were selected for the *O Henry Memorial Prize Stories* publications and for the *Best American Short Stories* series. Still's children's book, *Jack and the Wonder Beans,* illustrated by Margot Tomes, was chosen by the *New York Times* as one of the Best Illustrated Books of the Year for 1977.

Still died April 28, 2001 at age 94. He is buried on the campus of his beloved Hindman Settlement School at Hindman, Kentucky.

## Sources

Hewlett, Jennifer and Art Jester. "James Still, Appalachian Writer Dies: Former Kentucky Poet Laureate Inspired Generations of Kentucky Writers." *Lexington Herald Leader* Sunday 29 April 2001. Online. Accessed 3 Aug. 2014. <http://www.kentuckystewarts.com/RowanCounty/JamesStillAppalachianwriterdies.htm>.

"James Still Autobiography." *Contemporary Authors Autobiography Series* (17), Gale Research, 231-248.

"James Still: Biography." Famous People.com. Online. Accessed 2 Aug. 2014. <http://www.fampeople.com/cat-james-still>.

"James Still Homepage." Maintained by Sandy Hudock, Colorado State University-Pueblo, Pueblo, CO. Online. Accessed 2 Aug. 2014. <http://www.faculty.colostate-pueblo.edu/sandy.hudock/jshome.html>.

"James Still." *Kentucky in American Letters: Volume*
   *III 1913-1975*. Ed. Dorothy Edwards Townsend. Georgetown,
   KY: Georgetown College P, 1976. 319-322. Print.

Lyon, George Ella. "James Still Biography." *Kentucky*
   *Educational Television*. Online. Accessed 3 Aug. 2014.
   <http://www.ket.org/bookclub/books/2003_nov/bio.htm>.

Miller, Jim Wayne. "James Still." *The Kentucky Encyclopedia*.
   Ed. John Kleber. Lexington, KY: U P of Kentucky, 1992. 855-
   856. Print.

## Selected Bibliography

### Anecdotes & Tales

*Way down yonder on Troublesome Creek: Appalachian Riddles &*
   *Rusties*. New York: G. P. Putnam Sons, 1974. Print.

*The Wolfpen Rusties: Appalachian Riddles and Gee-Haw Whimmy-*
   *Diddles*. New York: G. P. Putnam Sons, 1975. Print.

### Children's Books

*Jack and the Wonder Beans*. New York: G. P. Putnam Sons, 1977. Print.

*An Appalachian Mother Goose*. Lexington, KY: U P of Kentucky,
   1998. Print.

### Collections

*The Wolfpen Notebooks: A Record of Appalachian Life* (Short
   Story, Poems, Appalachian Sayings). Lexington, KY: U P of
   Kentucky, 1991.

### Novels

*River of Earth*. New York: The Viking Press, 1940. Print.

*Sporty Creek: A Novel about an Appalachian Boyhood*. New
   York: G. P. Putnam Sons, 1977. Print.

*Chinaberry* (published posthumously). Ed. Silas House.
   Lexington, KY: U P of Kentucky, 2011. Print.

### Poetry

*Hounds on the Mountain*. New York: Viking Press, 1937. Print.

*The Wolfpen Poems*. Berea, KY: Berea College P, 1986. Print.

*From the Mountain, From the Valley: New and Collected Poems*
(published posthumously). Lexington, KY: U P of Kentucky,
2001. Print.

**Short Fiction**

*On Troublesome Creek.* New York: Viking Press, 1941. Print.

*Pattern of a Man.* Frankfort, KY: Gnomon Press, 1976. Print

*The Run for the Elbertas.* Lexington, KY: U P of Kentucky, 1980. Print.

*The Hills Remember: The Complete Short Stories of James Still*
(published posthumously). Ed. Ted Olson. Lexington, KY: U P
of Kentucky, 2012. Print.

# Robert Penn Warren

## 1905-1989

Guthrie, Kentucky native Robert Penn Warren is the only Kentucky author to win the Pulitzer Prize three times, and in two different genres. He won in 1947 for the novel *All the King's Men* and for two books of poetry— in 1948 for *Promises: Poems, 1954-1956* and again in 1979 for *Now and Then: Poems, 1976-1978*. *All the King's Men* was made into a play, a motion picture (three times), and an opera. The novel was eventually translated into twenty languages. Warren wrote ten novels, beginning in 1939 and ending in 1977. *Band of Angels* was also produced as a movie.

Critic Charles Bohmer says:

*Warren's ten novels are unified in both locale and theme. They are works about the South and southerners and, while aspiring to transcend their time and place, are nonetheless marked by a southern particularity that is deliberate, insistent, and unmistakable. They fall into two groups: the first group is historical and evokes a lost world recaptured through the imaginative use of documentary evidence; the second group is contemporary and constitutes a history of Warren's own times.*

Warren authored and published 16 books of poetry, beginning in 1936 and ending in 1985. He also published two collections of short stories, three children's books, four textbooks, six collections of essays, three historical works, one play, and one biography.

Literary critic Dwight Garner of the *New York Times* said of Warren's Pulitzer Prize winning novel *All the King's Men*:

*All the King's Men is a powerfully bleak novel; many lives are ruined over the course of it. Burden [a former political reporter who is Governor Willie Stark's right-hand man] is a student of ruin, a poet of it. 'There is a kind of snobbery of failure,' he thinks. 'It's a club, it's the old school, it's Skull and Bones.' Stark's failures are on a grander moral scale... All the King's Men is a sophisticated and even sensual novel about the breakdown of a kind of moral order. It's about the breaking of things that— as the nursery rhyme goes— can't be put back together again.*

Warren was a poet, critic, novelist, and teacher. He taught at Vanderbilt University, Southwestern College, University of Minnesota, Yale University, and Louisiana State University. He was appointed the nation's first Poet Laureate, February 26, 1986.

Warren was born in Todd County, Kentucky in the town of Guthrie. He entered Vanderbilt University at the age of 16. In 1925, he graduated *summa cum laude*, Phi Beta Kappa, and as a recipient of the Founder's Medal. He received his M.A. from the University of California in 1927, and did post graduate work at Yale University the following year. He was awarded a B. Litt. from Oxford University in 1930. Warren died September 15, 1989 and is buried at the Swills Cemetery in Stratton, Vermont.

**Sources**

Bohner, Charles. "Robert Penn Warren's Life and Career." *Modern American Poetry*. Online. Accessed 27 Jul. 2014. <http://www.english.illinois.edu/maps/poets/s_z/warren/life htm>.

Gardner, Dwight. *The New York Times* 11 April 2016. Online. Accessed 6 February 2016. <https://www.nytimes.com/2016/04/12/books/all-the-kings-men-now70-has-a-touch-of-2016.html?_r=0>.

Goode, James B. "Robert Penn Warren." *Kentucky's Twelve Days of Christmas*. Frankfort, KY: *Kentucky Monthly*, 2012. 24. Print.

Miller, Mary Ellen. "Robert Penn Warren." *The Kentucky Encyclopedia*. Ed. John Kleber. Lexington, Ky.: U P of Kentucky, 1992. 932. Print.

"Robert Penn Warren." *Kentucky in American Letters: Volume III 1913-1975*. Ed. Dorothy Edwards Townsend. Georgetown, KY: Georgetown College P, 1976. 382-385. Print.

"Robert Penn Warren (1905-1989)." Online. Accessed 27 Jul.
2014. <http://www.robertpennwarren.com/biography.htm>.

## Selected Bibliography
**Biography**
*John Brown: The Making of a Martyr*. New York: Payson & Clarke,
1929. Print.
**Children's Books**
*Remember the Alamo*. New York: Random House, 1958. Print.
*The Gods of Mount Olympus*. New York: Random House, 1959. Print.
*How Texas Won Her Freedom*. La Porte, TX: San Jacinto Museum of
History, 1959. Print.
**Collections**
*A Robert Penn Warren Reader*. New York: Random House, 1987. Print.
**Essays**
*Homage to Theodore Dreiser, On the Centennial of His Birth*, New
York: Random House, 1971. Print.
*John Greenleaf Whittier's Poetry: An Appraisal and a Selection*.
Minneapolis, MN: University of Minnesota P, 1971.
Print.
*Selected Essays*. New York: Random House, 1958. Print.
*Portrait of a Father*. Lexington, KY: U P of Kentucky, 1988.
Print.
*Jefferson Davis Gets His Citizenship Back*. Lexington, KY:
U P of Kentucky. 1980. Print.
*New and Selected Essays*. New York: Random House, 1989. Print.
**Historical Works**
*Segregation: The Inner Conflict in the South*. New York: Random
House, 1956. Print.
*The Legacy of the Civil War: Meditations on the Centennial*. New
York: Random House, 1961. Print.
*Who Speaks for the Negro*. New York: Random House, 1965. Print.
**Novels**
*Night Rider*. New York: Houghton-Mifflin, 1939. Print.

*At Heaven's Gate*. New York: Houghton-Mifflin, I943. Print.

*All the King's Men* (Pulitzer Prize). New York: Houghton-Mifflin, 1946. Print.

*World Enough and Time*. New York: Random House, 1950. Print.

*Band of Angels*. New York: Random House, 1955. Print.

*The Cave*. New York: Random House, 1959. Print.

*Wilderness: A Tale of the Civil War*. New York: Random House, 1961. Print.

*Flood: A Romance of Our Time*. New York: Random House, 1964. Print.

*Meet Me in the Green Glen*. New York: Random House, 1971. Print.

*A Place to Come To*. New York: Random House, 1977. Print.

**Poetry**

*Thirty-six Poems*. New York: Alcestis Press, 1936. Print.

*Eleven Poems on the Same Theme*. Norfolk, VA: New Directions, 1942. Print.

*Selected Poems: 1923-1943*. New York: Harcourt Brace, 1944. Print.

*Brother to Dragons: A Tale in Verse and Voices*. New York: Random House, 1953. Print.

*Promises: Poems 1954-1956* (*Pulitzer Prize*). New York: Random House, 1957. Print.

*You, Emperors, and Others: Poems 1957-1960*. New York: Random House, 1960. Print.

*Selected Poems: New and Old, 1923-1966*. New York: Random House, 1966. Print.

*Incarnations: Poems 1966-1968*. New York: Random House, 1968. Print.

*Audubon: A Vision*. New York: Random House, 1969. Print.

*Or Else: Poem/Poems 1968-1974*. New York: Random House, 1974. Print.

*Selected Poems: 1923-1976*. New York: Random House, 1977. Print.

*Now and Then: Poems 1976-1978* (Pulitzer Prize). New York: Random House, 1978. Print.

*Being Here: Poetry 1977-1980.* New York: Random House, 1980.
Print.

*Brother to Dragons: A Tale in Verse and Voices—A New Version.*
New York: Random House, 1979. Print.

*Rumor Verified: Poems 1979-1980.* New York: Random House, 1981.
Print.

*Chief Joseph of the Nez Perce.* New York: Random House, 1983.
Print.

*New & Selected Poems: 1923-1985.* New York: Random House, 1985.
Print.

**Plays**

*All the King's Men: A Play.* New York: Dramatists Play Service,
Inc., 1960. Print

**Short Stories**

*The Circus in the Attic, and Other Stories.* New York: Harcourt
Brace, 1947. Print.

*Blackberry Winter.* Cummington, MA: Cummington Press, 1946.
Print.

**Textbooks**

*Understanding Poetry* (with Cleanth Brooks). New York: Holt
Rinehart and Winston, 1938. Print.

*Understanding Fiction* (with Cleanth Brooks). New York: Appleton-
Century-Crofts, 1943. Print.

*Fundamentals of Good Writing - A Handbook of Modern Rhetoric*
(with Cleanth Brooks). New York: Harcourt Brace, 1950.
Print.

*American Literature: The Makers and the Making* (with Cleanth
Brooks and R.W.B. Lewis). New York: St. Martin's Press,
1974. Print.

# CHAPTER TWO
## 2014

# Rebecca Caudill Ayars

## 1899-1985

Harlan County, Kentucky native Rebecca Caudill Ayars is perhaps one of Kentucky's best known children's writers, having published more than twenty-three books between 1934 and 1985. Caudill was born February 2, 1899 and grew up as the middle child in a family of ten who lived at Poor Fork, Kentucky (now the city of Cumberland) in Harlan County. After her family moved to Tennessee, she worked her way through Wesleyan College in Macon, Georgia where she received an A.B. degree in 1920. She was the first in her family to attend college.

She taught English and History at Summer County High School in Portland, Tennessee from 1920-21. In 1922, she earned a Master's degree in international relations from Vanderbilt University. She taught English as a Second Language at Collegio Bennett in Rio de Janeiro for a short time. She also worked as an editor for the Methodist Publishing House in Nashville, Tennessee.

Caudill moved to Chicago for a another position with a publishing house, where she met and married James Sterling Ayars in 1931. In 1937, they moved with their two children, Jimmy and Becky Jean, to Urbana, Illinois where James took a job as the editor of the *Illinois Natural History Survey* at the University of Illinois campus.

Her first book *Barrie and Daughter* (1943), was a juvenile fiction novel based in part on her experiences growing up in rural Kentucky and Tennessee. *Tree of Freedom* (1949) was runner-up for the Newbery Award in 1950 and was selected as a *New York Herald Tribune* Honor Book the same year. *A Pocketful of Cricket* (1964) was a Caldecott Honor Book in 1965. She was also the recipient of the Hans Christian Anderson Award. Six of her books were Junior Literary Guild selections.

She published 18 books for children, one book of children's verse, a memoir/history *Appalachia: A Reminiscence* (1966), and three other non-fiction works. *Child of Appalachia* (1978), a film on her life and writing, was judged one of the top three entries at the Birmingham International Film Festival. The Rebecca Caudill Public Library in her hometown of Cumberland, Kentucky (formerly known as Poor Fork) was named in her honor. Rebecca Caudill Ayars died October 2, 1985 at the age of 86 and is buried in Mount Hope Cemetery and Mausoleum at Urbana, Illinois.

## Sources

"FantasticFiction: Rebecca Caudill." *FantasticFiction Company*.
Online. Accessed 30 Jul. 2014.
<http://www.fantasticfiction.co.uk/c/rebecca-caudill/happy-
little-family.htm>.

Kelly, JoAnne. "An Honest, Simple Life: A Biography of Rebecca
Caudill." *Champaign Public Library*. Online. Accessed 30 Jul.
2014.
<http://www.champaign.org/justkids/good_books/rebecca_ca
udill_award/meet_rebecca_caudill.html>.

"Rebecca Caudill." *The Kentucky Encyclopedia*. Ed. John Kleber.
Lexington, Ky.: U P of Kentucky, 1992. 173. Print.

"Rebecca Caudill." *Kentucky in American Letters: Volume III
1913-1975*. Ed. Dorothy Edwards Townsend. Georgetown,
KY: Georgetown College P, 1976. 52-54. Print.

"Rebecca Caudill Bio." *Young Readers Book Award*. Online.
Accessed 30 Jul. 2014. <http://www.rcyrba.org/Rebecca-
CaudillBio.htm>.

## Selected Bibliography

### Biographical

*Florence Nightingale*. New York: Harper & Row, 1953. Print.

### Collections

*Contrary Jenkins*. New York: Holt, Rinehart, Winston, 1969.
Print.

*Home for Christmas: Stories for Young & Old* (with Pearl Buck
et al). Farmington, PA: Plough Publishing House, 2002.
Print.

### Children's Picture Books

*Higgins and the Great Big Scare*. New York: Holt, Rinehart,
Winston, 1960. Print.

*The Best Loved Doll*. New York: Holt, Rinehart, Winston, 1962. Print.

*A Pocket Full of Cricket*. New York: Henry Holt & Company, 1964.
Print.

*A Certain Small Shepherd*. New York: Holt, Rinehart, Winston, 1965. Print.

*Did You Carry the Flag Today Charley?* New York: Henry Holt & Company, 1966. Print.

**Children's Series: The Fairchild Family Story**

*Happy Little Family*. Philadelphia: The John C. Winston Company, 1947. Print.

*Schoolhouse in the Woods*. Philadelphia: The John C. Winston Company, 1949. Print.

*Up and Down the River*. Philadelphia: The John C. Winston Company, 1951. Print.

*Schoolroom in the Parlor*. Philadelphia: The John C. Winston Company, 1959. Print.

**Non-Fiction**

*My Appalachia: A Reminiscence*. New York: Holt, Rinehart, Winston, 1966. Print.

*Come Along*. New York: Holt, Rinehart, Winston, 1969. Print.

*Wind, Sand, & Sky*. New York: E. P. Dutton, 1976. Print.

**Novels**

*Barrie & Daughter*. New York: Viking Press, 1942. Print.

*Tree of Freedom*. New York: Viking Press, 1947. Print.

*Saturday Cousins*. Philadelphia: John C. Winston Company, 1953. Print.

*House of the Fifers*. New York: David McKay Company, 1954. Print.

*Susan Cornish*. New York: Viking Press, 1955. Print.

*Time for Lissa*. New York: Thomas Nelson, & Sons, 1959. Print.

*The Far Off Land*. New York: Viking Press, 1964. Print.

*Somebody Go and Bang a Drum*. New York: Dutton, 1974. Print.

# Thomas D. Clark
## 1903-2005

Native Mississippian Thomas Dionysius Clark was Kentucky's most well-known and accomplished academic historian. He was known as a superb professor, passionate preservationist, consummate lecturer, dynamic public speaker, dedicated researcher, and skilled writer. Clark devoted his life to the preservation of Kentucky's historical records. He collected vast stores of Kentucky's military records from the War of 1812, the Mexican War, and the Civil War. His tireless efforts resulted in the Commonwealth's first archival system and the subsequent creation of the Kentucky Library and Archives, the University of Kentucky Special Collections and Archives, the Kentucky Oral

History Commission, The Thomas Clark Kentucky History Center, and the University Press of Kentucky.

Dr. Clark dropped out of school after seventh grade to work first at a sawmill and then on a canal dredge boat, before realizing he needed to resume his formal education. Clark enrolled in high school soon afterwards. His account of that was recorded in an interview:

> *I left the boat in September 1920. Without a job. Without a future, really. I accidentally met a boy who told me about an agricultural high school Choctaw County Agricultural High School. I went down and within 10 minutes of getting off the train I'd registered. The old superintendent didn't ask me one thing about my education. He didn't know if I could read or write. Said you look like a big stout boy. You look like you'd make a good football player. So I was admitted as a football player. I went to that school for four years [and obtained] reasonably basic preparation.*

He earned his bachelor's degree (with honors) from the University of Mississippi (1928), a Master's Degree from the University of Kentucky (1929), and a Doctorate from Duke University (1932).

He taught history at the University of Kentucky for thirty-seven years and served twenty-three years as Department Chair, until he retired from the University in 1968. He also served as a visiting professor at Harvard University, Duke University, Stanford University, University of Wisconsin, University of Tennessee, University of Washington, and The University of Chicago.

Clark authored or edited over thirty-six books on a wide variety of historical topics. His most popular book was *A History of Kentucky* (1937), which is considered one of the state's best histories ever published. This seminal work is still in print, as are many of his great works. In 1990, the Kentucky General Assembly named Clark Kentucky Historian Laureate for life. Kentucky Governor Brereton Jones called him "Kentucky's greatest treasure." Clark's honors included several awards for his writing, a Guggenheim fellowship and eight honorary degrees.

He was active in professional organizations, serving as president of the Southern Historical Association (1947) and as editor of the *Journal of Southern History* (1949–52). Later, he was served as president of the Organization of American Historians (1956–57) and as executive secretary (1970–73). He received the AHA's Award for Scholarly Distinction in 2004.

He married Mary Elizabeth Turner on June 10, 1933 and they were together until her death in 1955. His first marriage produced two children, Elizabeth and Bennett. In 1996, he married Loretta Gilliam and they were together until his death in June 2005, a few days short of his 102nd birthday. Dr. Clark is buried in the Lexington Cemetery at Lexington, Kentucky.

James Klotter, another great Kentucky historian, said of Clark upon his death: "He will be remembered as a person who took history to the people and didn't just stay in an ivy-covered tower somewhere writing books in the dark of the night, but got out and taught history all across the commonwealth. All across the world really."

## Sources

Mead, Andy. "Thomas D. Clark 1903-2005." *The Lexington Herald Leader* 28 June 2005. Print.

"My Century in History." *OpenISBN*. Online. Accessed 13 Aug. 2014. <http://www.openisbn.com/isbn/9780813124001/>.

"Thomas D. Clark, 'historical conscience,' Dies." *Cincinnati.com* 29 July 2005. Online. Accessed 13 Aug. 2014. <http://www.cincinnati.com/apps/pbcs.dll/article?AID=/20050 629/NEWS0104/506290373/1060/NEWS01>.

"Thomas D. Clark." *Kentucky in American Letters: Volume III 1913-1975*. Ed. Dorothy Edwards Townsend. Georgetown, KY: Georgetown College P, 1976. 67-69. Print.

"Thomas D. Clark 1903-2005." *Perspectives on History: The Newsmagazine of the National Historical Association* Oct. 2005. Online. Accessed 13 Aug. 2014. <https://www.historians.org/publications-and-directories/perspectives-on-history/october-2005/in-memoriam-thomas-d-clark>.

Wallace, H. Lew. "Thomas Dionysius Clark." *The Kentucky Encyclopedia*. Ed. John Kleber. Lexington, Ky.: U P of Kentucky, 1992. 196-197. Print.

## Selected Bibliography

### Edited

*Bluegrass Cavalcade*. Lexington, KY: University of Kentucky P, 1956. Print.

*Travels in the Old South*. Norman, OK: University of Oklahoma P, 1956. Print.

*Travels in the New South*. Norman, OK: University of Oklahoma P, 1962. Print.

*Gold Rush Diary: The Diary of E. Douglas Perkins*. Lexington, KY: University of Kentucky P, 1967. Print.

*Off at Sunrise, The Diary of Charles Glass Gray*. San Marino, CA: California Huntington Library, 1976. Print.

*The Voice of the Frontier: John Bradford's Notes on Kentucky.*
Lexington, KY: U P of Kentucky, 1993. Print.

**Historical/Social Commentary**

*Beginning of the L&N, From New Orleans to Cairo.* Chicago, IL:
The Illinois Central Railroad, 1933. Print.

*A Pioneer Southern Railroad from New Orleans to Cairo.* Chapel
Hill, NC: University of North Carolina P, 1936. Print.

*A History of Kentucky.* New York: Prentice Hall, 1937. Print.

*The Rampaging Frontier: Manners and Humors of Pioneer Days in
the South and Middle West.* Indianapolis, IN: Bobbs-Merrill,
1939. Print.

*Exploring Kentucky.* New York: The American Book Company, 1939.
Print.

*The Kentucky (Rivers of America Series).* New York: Farrar &
Rinehart, 1942. Print.

*Simon Kenton, Kentucky Scout.* New York: Farrar & Rinehart, 1943.
Print.

*Pills, Petticoats, and Plows: The Southern Country Store.*
Indianapolis, IN: Bobbs-Merrill, 1944. Print.

*Southern Country Editor.* Indianapolis, IN: Bobbs-Merrill, 1948. Print.

*The Rural Press and the New South.* Baton Rouge: Louisiana State
U P, 1948. Print.

Clark, Thomas and A.D. Kirwan. *The Emerging South.* New York:
Oxford University P, 1961. Print.

*The South Since Appomattox.* New York: Oxford University P,
1967. Print.

*Kentucky, Land of Contrast.* New York: Harper & Row, 1968. Print.

*Three American Frontiers. Writings of Thomas D. Clark.*
Lexington, KY: University of Kentucky P, 1968. Print.

*Pleasant Hill and Its Shakers.* Pleasant Hill, KY: Shakertown
Press, 1968. Print.

*Agrarian Kentucky.* Lexington, KY: The U P of Kentucky, 1977. Print.

*History of Indiana University* (4 volumes). Bloomington, IN:
Indiana University P, 1970. Print.

*Pleasant Hill in the Civil War*. Pleasant Hill, KY: Pleasant Hill
    Press, 1972. Print.
*South Carolina, The Grand Tour. 1780-1865*. Columbia, SC:
    University of South Carolina P, 1973. Print.
*A Century of Banking History in the Bluegrass: The Second
    National Bank and Trust Company*. Lexington, KY: John
    Bradford Press, 1983. Print.
*What I Saw in California* (with Edwin Bryant). Lincoln, NE: The
    University of Nebraska Press, 1985. Print.
*Frontiers in Conflict: The Old West*. 1795-1830. Albuquerque,
    NM: University of New Mexico P, 1989. Print.
*Footloose in Jacksonian America: Robert W. Scott and His
    Agrarian World*. Frankfort, KY: The Kentucky Historical
    Society, 1989. Print.
*Kentucky Bluegrass Country* (*Folklife in the South Series* with
    Gerald Alvey). Jackson, MS: The U of Mississippi P, 1992. Print.
*Clark County, Kentucky, A History*. Winchester, KY: Winchester
    Clark County Heritage Commission, 1995. Print.
*The Old Southwest, 1795-1830: Frontiers in Conflict*. Norman, OK:
    The University of Oklahoma P, 1996. Print.
*The People's House: Governor's Mansions of Kentucky* (with
    Margaret A. Lane). Lexington, KY: U P of Kentucky, 2002.
    Print.
*Restoring Shakertown. The Struggle to Save the Historic Shaker
    Village of Pleasant Hill*. Lexington, KY: U P of Kentucky, 2005.
    Print.
*My Century in History: Memoirs*. Lexington, KY: U P of Kentucky,
    2006. Print.
*Bluegrass Cavalcade*. Lexington, KY: U P of Kentucky, 2009. Print.

# Janice Holt Giles
## 1905-1979

Altus, Arkansas native Janice Holt Giles did not begin her first novel until 1946 when she was 41 years of age and did not finish it until four years later. She wrote *Enduring Hills* (1950), a historical fiction novel, while employed full-time as a secretary for Dr. Louis Sherrill, Dean of the Louisville Presbyterian Theological Seminary.

Janice married her first husband Otto Moore in 1927 and divorced him in 1939. She met an Army Sergeant Henry Giles on a bus ride in 1943. They corresponded during World War II and were married in 1945, after Henry was discharged from the Army. In 1946, they moved near Henry's ancestral land at

Knifley, Kentucky in Adair County.

Between 1950 and 1975 she wrote twenty-six books, most of which were bestsellers. Her books were regularly reviewed in the *New York Times* and selected for inclusion by popular book clubs. She published close to a book-per-year from 1950-1975; some years publishing multiple books — three in 1951, and two in 1954. These included 19 novels, six non-fiction works, and one collection of both fiction and non-fiction. There are numerous reports that her collective sales exceeded three million copies.

One critic wrote, "In her historical novels about Kentucky, Janice Holt Giles has become known for the integrity with which she handles her material and for the realism with which she writes." Janice's biographer, Dianne Watkins Stuart in her book *Janice Holt Giles: A Writer's Life* (1998) found that "Her picture held pride of place in her literary agent's New York office alongside those of Willa Cather, H.G. Wells, and Edith Wharton."

Giles's historical fiction depicts early American pioneer life and covers a wide range of geography, including Kentucky, Tennessee, Virginia, Arkansas, Oklahoma, Texas, and New Mexico. Her historical figures include Daniel Boone, Sam Houston, James Harrod, and others. One critic suggested that at the core of her work is a certain democracy in depicting the complexity of relationships between White Settlers, Native Americans, and African Americans.

Stuart revealed that Giles often humbly professed to be "just a good storyteller" but that she was much more; she was a keen and sensitive observer of life, with a good ear for language, and a superb imagination.

Janice died in 1979 and her husband, Henry Giles, in 1986. Both are buried in the Caldwell Chapel Separate Baptist

Church Cemetery at Knifley, Kentucky.

**Sources**

Cox, Bonnie Jean. "Janice Holt Giles." *The Kentucky Encyclopedia*. Ed. John Kleber. Lexington, KY: U P of Kentucky, 1992. 374. Print.

"Janice Holt Giles." Findagrave.com. Online. Accessed 4 Aug. 2014. <http://www.findagrave.com/cgi- bin/ fg.cgi?page=gr&GRid=78550270>.

"Janice Holt Giles." *Kentucky in American Letters: Volume III 1913-1975*. Ed. Dorothy Edwards Townsend. Georgetown, KY: Georgetown College P, 1976. 126-128. Print.

"Janice Holt Giles and Henry Giles Society." Online. Accessed 4 Aug. 2014. <http://www.gilessociety.org/>.

Plemmons, Florence Williams. "Janice Holt Giles: A Bio-Bibliography with Evaluations of the Kentucky Frontier Books as Historical Fiction." Master's Thesis: University of Tennessee. 1969. Online. Accessed 16 Aug. 2014. <http://trace.tennessee.edu/cgi/viewcontent.cgi?article=2233 &context=utk_gradthes&sei- edir=1&referer=http%3A%2F%2Fwww. bing.com %2Fsearch%3Fq%3Djanice%2 Bholt%2Bgiles%2 Bbibliograpy%26qs%3DHS%26pq%3Djanice%2Bholt%2Bgil es%2Bbiblio%26sc%3D1- 24%26sp%3D1%26cvid%3Db5f682dccff94653a4242124763 e5dda%26FORM%3DQBRE#search=%22janice%20holt%20 giles%20bibliograpy%22>.

Stuart, Dianne Watkins. *Janice Holt Giles: A Writer's Life*. Lexington, KY: The U P of Kentucky, 1998. Print.

**Selected Bibliography**
**Collections (Fiction & Non-Fiction)**
*Wellspring*. Boston: Houghton Mifflin, 1975. Print.

**Novels**

*The Enduring Hills*. Philadelphia: Westminster Press, 1950. Print.

*Miss Willie*. Philadelphia: Westminster Press, 1951. Print.

*Tara's Healing*. Philadelphia: Westminster Press, 1951. Print.

*Harbin's Ridge* (with Henry Giles). Boston: Houghton Mifflin, 1951. Print.

*The Kentuckians*. Boston: Houghton Mifflin, 1953. Print.

*The Plum Thicket*. Boston: Houghton Mifflin, 1954. Print.

*Hill Man* (using pseudonym John Garth). New York: Pyramid Books, 1954. Print.

*Hannah Fowler*. Boston: Houghton Mifflin, 1956. Print.

*The Believers*. Boston: Houghton Mifflin, 1957. Print.

*Land Beyond the Mountains*. Boston: Houghton Mifflin, 1958. Print.

*Johnny Osage*. Boston: Houghton Mifflin, 1960. Print.

*Savanna*. Boston: Houghton Mifflin, 1961. Print.

*Voyage to Santa Fe*. Boston: Houghton Mifflin, 1962. Print.

*Run Me a River*. Boston: Houghton Mifflin, 1964. Print.

*The Great Adventure*. Boston: Houghton Mifflin, 1966. Print.

*Shady Grove*. Boston: Houghton Mifflin, 1967. Print.

*Six Horse Hitch*. Boston: Houghton Mifflin, 1969. Print.

*Act of Contrition*. Lexington, KY: U P of Kentucky, 2001. Print.

**Non-Fiction**

*Forty Acres and No Mule*. Philadelphia: Westminster Press, 1952. Print.

*A Little Better Than Plumb* (with Henry Giles). Boston: Houghton Mifflin, 1963. Print.

*The G.I. Journal of Sergeant Giles* (with Henry Giles). Boston: Houghton Mifflin, 1965. Print.

*The Damned Engineers*. Boston: Houghton Mifflin, 1970. Print.

*Around Our House* (with Henry Giles). Boston: Houghton Mifflin, 1971. Print.

*The Kinta Years*. Boston: Houghton Mifflin, 1973. Print.

Photograph by Louis Bickett.

# James Baker Hall

## 1935-2009

Lexington, Kentucky native James Baker Hall was a versatile writer, having excelled as a poet, novelist, short story writer, and photographer. He was also a consummate teacher, having taught for over thirty years (1973-2003) in the University of Kentucky English Department, where he also served as Director of the Creative Writing Program.

Hall was a member of the "Fabulous Five," that was taught creative writing by noted novelist and poet Robert Hazel at the University of Kentucky along with fellow students that included: Bobbie Ann Mason, Wendell Berry, Gurney Norman, and Ed McClanahan. Hall once said that Hazel encouraged his students to "escape the provincialism of their heritage" by leaving Kentucky. Hall did just that, living in Paris, France and on both coasts of the United States. Hall also studied at Stanford University as a Stegner Fellow in the 1960s alongside Larry McMurty and Ken Kesey.

Before coming to the University of Kentucky, Hall taught poetry and photography at Massachusetts Institute of Technology in the early 1970s. He was fond of telling the story that the Department at MIT needed a poetry teacher and he began teaching the course without ever having written a poem. He went on to become one of the most accomplished poets in Kentucky, eventually serving as the Commonwealth's Poet Laureate (2001-2002). He also lectured at the Rhode Island School of Design, The Visual Workshop, and the Minneapolis Museum of Art. Hall became close colleagues with such accomplished photographers as Minor White, Richard Benson, and Ralph Eugene Meatyard. He served as contributing editor for the prestigious photography magazine *Aperture*.

Hall authored several volumes of poetry including *Stopping on the Edge to Wave* (1988), *Fast Signing Mute* (1992), *The Mother on the Other Side of the World* (1999), and *The Total Light Process: New & Selected Poems* (2004). He was the author of a novel-in-verse, *Praeder's Letters* (2002). His poems have been published in *The New Yorker*, *The Paris Review*, *Poetry*, *The American Poetry Review*, *The Kenyon Review*, and elsewhere.

He received his B.A. from the University of Kentucky (1957) and his M.A. at Stanford University (1961). He studied under such luminaries as Malcolm Cowley and Frank O'Connor. Hall received an NEA Fellowship in Poetry (1980), won the Pushcart Prize (1983) and O Henry Prize (1967). Additionally, he was awarded a Southern Arts Federation Photography Fellowship (1993) and a Kentucky Arts Council Al Smith Fellowship (1986).

Hall died in his home at Sadieville, Kentucky in 2009 at age 74. Hundreds attended his memorial service held at the Carnegie Center in Lexington, Kentucky July 11, 2009.

## Sources

Cheves, John. "Hundreds Memorialize James Baker Hall." *The Lexington Herald Leader*. 12 July 2009. Online. Accessed 6 Aug. 2014. <http://www.kentucky.com/2009/07/12/860090/hundreds-memorialize-james-baker.html>.

"Five Kentucky Poet Laureates: An Anthology: James Baker Hall." *The Kentucky Arts Council*. Online. Accessed 6 Aug. 2014. <http://artscouncil.ky.gov/Resources/PA_Hall.htm>.

"James Baker Hall." *James Baker Hall Archive*. Online. Accessed 6 Aug. 2014. <http://jamesbakerhall.com/about_bio.htm>.

"Living By Words: James Baker Hall, A Profile." Interview by Guy Mendes. *KET* 28 Nov. 2001. Online. Accessed 6 Aug. 2014. <http://www.ket.org/livingbywords/authors/hall.htm>.

## Selected Bibliography

**Anthologies:**

*Stanford Short Stories*. Eds. Wallace Stegner and Richard Scowcroft. Redwood City, CA: Stanford University P, 1962. Print.

*Prize Stories 1968 The O. Henry Awards*. Ed. William Abrahams. New York: Doubleday & Co., 1968. Print.

*Kentucky Renaissance: An Anthology of Contemporary Writing*. Ed. Jonathon Greene. Frankfort, KY: Gnomon Press: Kentucky, 1976. Print.

*50 Contemporary Poets: The Creative Process*. Ed. Alberta T. Turner. Philadelphia, PA: David McKay Company, Inc., 1977. Print.

*Traveling America with Today's Poets*. Ed. David Kherdian. New York: Macmillan Publishing Co., 1977. Print.

*The Pushcart Prize, VIII: Best of the Small Presses*. Ed. Bill
  Henderson. New York: The Pushcart Press, 1983-1984. Print.
*Home Ground: Southern Autobiography*. Ed. J. Bill Berry.
  Columbia, MO: University of Missouri P, 1991. Print.

**Novels**

*Yates Paul, His Grand Flights, His Tootings*. Cleveland,
  OH: World Publishing Co., 1963.
_____ (reprint). London, UK: Cassell & Co., 1964
_____ (reprint). Lexington, KY: U P of Kentucky, 2002. Print.
*Praeder's Letters* (novel in verse). Louisville, KY: Sarabande
  Books, 2002. Print.

**Photography**

*Ralph Eugene Meatyard*. New York: Aperture, 1974. Print.
*Minor White: Rites and Passages*. New York: Aperture, 1978. Print.
*Orphan in the Attic*. Lexington, KY: University of Kentucky Art
  Museum, 1995. Print.
*A Spring-Fed Pond*. Kentucky: Crystal Publications, 2000. Print.
*Tobacco Harvest: An Elegy*. Lexington, KY: U P of Kentucky, 2004. Print.

**Poetry**

*Getting it on Up to the Brag*. Monterey, KY: Larkspur Press, 1975. Print.
*Her Name*. Marqesan, WI: Pentagram Press, 1982. Print.
*Music for a Broken Piano*. Brooklyn, NY: Fiction Collective, 1982. Print.
*Stopping on the Edge to Wave*. Middletown, CT: Wesleyan U P, 1988.
  Print.
*Fast Signing Mute*. Monterey, KY: Larkspur Press, 1992. Print.
*The Mother on the Other Side of the World*. Louisville, KY:
  Sarabande Books, 1999. Print.
*The Total Light Process: New and Selected Poems*. Lexington, KY:
  U P of Kentucky, 2004. Print.
*Pleasure* (Poems & Photography). Carrollton, OH: Press on the
  Scroll Road, 2007. Print.

# Etheridge Knight
## 1931-1991

Etheridge Knight was a native of Corinth, Mississippi, born into a poor family of seven children. Knight spent most of his adolescent years working in pool halls, bars, and juke joints, where he developed a drug habit early in life. In these places, he learned an oral poetry form called "Toasts" which involved memorizing a long narrative poem that was then performed before audiences in the bars he frequented. This was a kind of mental gymnastics that showcased the artist's memorization and performance skills. His family spent a significant portion of Knight's adolescence in Paducah, Kentucky where his father worked on construction of Kentucky Dam, before the family moved to Indianapolis, Indiana.

He joined the U.S. Army in 1947, serving as a medical technician during the Korean War but was discharged in 1951 after suffering shrapnel wounds that deepened his drug addiction. He was arrested in Indianapolis for stealing a purse in 1960, convicted, and imprisoned at the Indiana State Prison for eight years. While in prison he continued his interest in the "Toasts" form, emerging as a poet who became the voice of the black aesthetic movement with his first volume of verse *Poems from Prison* (1968) and a prose anthology *Black Voices from Prison* (1970).

He married fellow poet Sonia Sanchez, following his release from prison, but they divorced two years later. He was married two other times, once to Mary Ann McAnally (with whom he had two children), and later to Charlene Blackburn (with whom he had one son). Knight taught at various universities and contributed to several magazines, working two years as an editor of *Motive* and as a contributing editor of *New Letters* (1974).

According to Shirley Lumpkin in the *Dictionary of Literary Biography*, "His work was hailed by black writers and critics as another excellent example of the powerful truth of blackness in art. His became important in Afro-American poetry and poetics and in Anglo-American poetry descended from Walt Whitman." Whereas, Walt Whitman said that the poet was a prophet, Knight suggested that the poet was a "meddler" who formed a trinity with the poem and the reader. Much of his verse was collected in *The Essential Etheridge Knight* (1986). In much of Knight's poetry, the thematic arc asserts that imprisonment of the black person constitutes a kind of extension of slavery.

In 1990, he earned a bachelor's degree in American poetry and criminal justice from Martin Center University in Indianapolis. He was nominated for a Pulitzer Prize in Poetry and the National Book Award for *Belly Songs and Other Poems* (1973).

He received a National Endowment for the Arts grant in 1972 and a Guggenheim Fellowship in 1974.

Knight was highly respected by such great poet/writers as Gwendolyn Brooks, Robert Bly, and Galway Kinnell. According to Lumpkin, this group considered him to be "... a major Afro-American poet because of his human subject matter, his combination of traditional techniques with an expertise in using rhythmic and oral speech patterns, and his ability to feel and to project his feelings into a poetic structure that moves others."

Etheridge died of lung cancer March 10, 1991 in Indianapolis, Indiana. He is buried at the Crown Hill Cemetery in Indianapolis.

### Sources

"Biography Etheridge Knight." *PoetandPoem.com*. Online. Accessed 13 Aug. 2014.
<http://www.poetandpoem.com/594_biography_of_poet_Etheridge_Knight.html>.

"Etheridge Knight." *PoemHunter.com*. Online. Accessed 13 August 2014. <http://www.poemhunter.com/etheridge-knight/biography/>.

"Etheridge Knight." *Poetry Foundation*. Online. Accessed 13 Aug. 2014.
<http://www.poetryfoundation.org/bio/etheridge-knight>.

"Etheridge Knight." *Answers*. Online. Accessed 13 Aug. 2014.
<http://www.answers.com/topic/etheridge-knight>.

Lumpkin, Shirley. "Etheridge Knight" *Dictionary of Literary Biography: Afro-American Poets since 1955*: 41 (1985). Detroit: Gale Research Company, 1985. Print.

## Selected Bibliography

### Collections (Poetry)

*Voce Negre dal Carcere* (et al). Laterza, Italy, 1968. Print.

*Black Voices from Prison* (et al). New York: Pathfinder Press, 1970. Print.

### Poetry

*A Poem for Brother/Man*. Detroit: Broadside Press, 1972. Print.

*Belly Song and Other Poems*. Detroit: Broadside Press, 1973. Print.

*Born of a Woman: New and Selected Poems*. Boston: Houghton Mifflin, 1980. Print.

*The Essential Etheridge Knight*. Pittsburgh: University of Pittsburgh P, 1986. Print.

# Thomas Merton

## 1915-1968

Although a native of Prades, France, Thomas Merton spent twenty-seven years in Nelson County, Kentucky as a Trappist Monk in the Abbey of Gethsemani. He authored over seventy books covering a wide range of genres including autobiography, biography, essays, poetry, novel, and letters. He wrote numerous poems and articles with a wide variety of topics: religious spirituality, non-violence, social justice, interfaith understanding, comparative religion, and nuclear proliferation.

Most notable of his publications were his best-selling autobiography *The Seven Storey Mountain* (1948) which sold over one million copies and has been translated into fifteen languages,

*Seeds of Contemplation* (1949), and *The Sign of Jonas* (1953). He published over 2,000 poems during his career. *The Collected Poems of Thomas Merton* was published posthumously (1977).

He is widely considered to be the most important American Catholic writer of the twentieth century. He was known as an activist who considered race and peace the two most urgent issues of his time. He was an ardent supporter of Martin Luther King, Jr. and the nonviolent civil rights movement, which he cited as being "... the greatest example of Christian faith in action in the social history of the United States."

During his writing career, he was considered to be at the forefront of a world-wide ecumenical movement. His role as a religious thinker and social critic is often compared to Dietrich Bonhoeffer, Flannery O'Connor, and Martin Luther King, Jr.

He attended Cambridge University for one year (1933). He entered Columbia University in January 1935 and graduated with a B.A. in English (1938). In late 1938, he made a religious conversion and was received into the Catholic Church at Corpus Christi Church. After graduation, he stayed at Columbia, taking graduate courses toward his M.A. In 1940, he completed his master's thesis "On Nature and Art in William Blake." While at Columbia, he studied under some remarkable teachers of literature, including Mark Van Doren, Daniel C. Walsh, and Joseph Wood Krutch. From 1940-1941 he taught English at St. Bonaventure College, a Catholic Franciscan school in Allegany, New York. In December 1941, he entered the Abbey of Our Lady of Gethsemani at New Haven, Kentucky as a Trappist Monk. He remained there for the next twenty-seven years until his accidental death from electrocution in 1968 in Bangkok, Thailand, while attending a conference of Asian Benedictines and Cistercians.

Merton is buried in the Monk's cemetery inside the Abbey of Gethsemani at Trappist, Kentucky and has a memorial site in the gardens outside the monastery.

## Sources

Artikel, Dieser. "Thomas Merton Bibliography." Online.
    Accessed 28 Jul. 2014.
    <http://en.potiori.com/Thomas_Merton_bibliography.html>.
"Biography of Thomas Merton." *Thomas Merton Society of Canada*.
    Online. Accessed 28 Jul. 2014.
    <http://www.merton.ca/biography.html>.
Daggy, Robert. "Thomas Merton." *The Kentucky Encyclopedia*.
    Ed. John Kleber. Lexington, KY: U P of Kentucky, 1992. 629.
    Print.
"Father Thomas Louis Merton." *Kentucky in American Letters:*
    *Volume III 1913-1975*. Ed. Dorothy Edwards Townsend.
    Georgetown, KY: Georgetown College P, 1976. 230-232.
    Print.
"Thomas Merton." *The Famous People: The Society for Recognition*
    *of Famous People*. Online. Accessed 28 Jul. 2014.
    <http://www.thefamouspeople.com/profiles/thomas-merton-
    268.php>.
"Thomas Merton's Life and Work." *The Thomas Merton Center at*
    *Bellarmine College*. Online. Accessed 28 Jul. 2014.
    <http://merton.org/chrono.aspx>.

## Selected Bibliography

### Autobiographies

*The Seven Storey Mountain*. New York: Harcourt Brace, 1948. Print.
*The Sign of Jonas*. New York: Harcourt Brace, 1953. Print.
*Day of a Stranger*. Salt Lake City, UT: Peregrine Smith, 1981. Print.

### Biblical Topics

*Bread in the Wilderness*. Norfolk, CT: New Directions, 1953. Print.

*The Living Bread*. New York: Farrar, Straus & Cudahy, 1956. Print.

*Praying the Psalms*. Collegeville, MN: The Liturgical Press, 1956. Print.

*He Is Risen*. Niles, IL: Argus Communications, 1973. Print.

## Bibliography/Letters

*On The Banks of Monk's Pond: The Thomas Merton/Jonathan Greene Correspondence, With Essays by Jonathan Greene*. Ed. Jonathan Greene. Frankfort, KY: Broadstone Books, 2004. Print.

Papagni, Mario. *The Cold War Letters of Thomas Merton*. M.A. Thesis: Spring Hill College, 2006. Print.

*Thomas Merton: A Life in Letters*. Eds. William H. Shannon and Christine M. Bochen. New York: HarperOne, 2008. Print.

*Thomas Merton: A Life in Letters*. Eds. William H. Shannon and Christine M. Bochen. Notre Dame, IN: Ave Maria Press, 2010. Print.

## Biographies

*Exile Ends in Glory: The Life of a Trappistine, Mother M. Berchmans, O.C.S.O.* Milwaukee, WI: Bruce Publishing Company, 1948. Print.

*What are These Wounds?: The Life of a Cistercian Mystic, Saint Lutgarde of Aywières*. Dublin/London: Clonmore and Reynolds, 1948. Print.

*The Last of the Fathers: Saint Bernard of Clairvaux and the Encyclical Letter, Doctor Mellifluus*. New York: Harcourt Brace, 1954. Print.

## Contemplation and Meditations

*Seeds of Contemplation*. Norfolk, CT: New Directions, 1949. Print.

*The Ascent to Truth*. New York: Harcourt Brace, 1951. Print.

*Disputed Questions*. New York: Farrar, Straus and Cudahy, 1960. Print.

*New Seeds of Contemplation*. London, UK: Burns & Oates, 1962. Print.

*Raids on the Unspeakable*. Norfolk, CT: New Directions, 1966. Print.

*Conjectures of a Guilty Bystander*. New York: Doubleday, 1966. Print.

*Contemplative Prayer*. New York: Herder and Herder, 1969. Print.
*Spiritual Direction and Meditation and What is Contemplation?*
    Weathampstead-Hertfordshire, UK: Anthony Clarke Books,
    1975. [1st published 1950]. Print.

**Eastern Thought**

*The Way of Chuang Tzu*. Norfolk, CT: New Directions, 1965. Print.
*Mystics and Zen Masters*. New York: Farrar, Straus and Giroux,
    1967. Print.
*Zen and the Birds of Appetite*. Norfolk, CT: New Directions,
    1968. Print.

**Essays & Misc.**

*The Behavior of Titans*. Norfolk, CT: New Directions. 1961. Print.
*Ishi means man* (foreword by Dorothy Day & woodblock by Rita
    Corbin). Greensboro, NC: Unicorn Press, 1976. Print.
Merton, Thomas and Patrick Hart. *The Literary Essays of Thomas
    Merton*. Norfolk, CT: New Directions, 1981. Print.
*Thomas Merton: Spiritual Master*. Ed. Laurence S. Cunningham.
    Mahwah, NJ: Paulist Press, 1992. Print.

**Journal Writings**

*The Secular Journal of Thomas Merton*. New York: Farrar, Straus &
    Cudahy, 1959. Print.
*The Asian Journal of Thomas Merton*. Norfolk, CT: New Directions,
    1973. Print.
*Woods, Shore and Desert: A Notebook, May 1968*. Santa Fe, NM:
    Museum of New Mexico P, 1982. Print.
*Cassian and the Fathers: Notes for Conferences Given in the
    Choir Novitiate. Abbey of Gethsemani*. New Haven, KY:
    Abbey of Gesthamni, 2005. Print.
*The Other Side of the Mountain: The End of the Journey; the
    Journals of Thomas Merton, Volume 7, 1967-1968*. New
    York: HarperOne, 1998. Print.

**Monastic, Church and Spiritual Life**

*The Waters of Siloe*. New York: Harcourt Brace, 1949. Print.
*No Man Is an Island*. New York: Harcourt Brace, 1955. Print.

*Silence in Heaven*. London, UK: Thames & Hudson, 1956. Print.

*The Silent Life*. New York: Farrar, Straus & Cudahy, 1957. Print.

*Thoughts in Solitude*. New York: Farrar, Straus & Cudahy, 1958. Print.

*The Wisdom of the Desert: Sayings From the Desert Fathers of
the Fourth Century*. Norfolk, CT: New Directions, 1960. Print.

*Spiritual Direction and Meditation*. Collegeville, MN:
Liturgical Press, 1960. Print.

*The New Man*. New York: Farrar, Straus & Cudahy, 1961. Print.

*Life and Holiness*. New York: Herder and Herder, 1963. Print.

*Seasons of Celebration*. New York: Farrar, Straus and Giroux,
1965. Print.

*Gethsemani: A Life of Praise*. New Haven, KY: Abbey of
Gethsemani, 1966. Print.

*Contemplation in a World of Action*. New York: Doubleday. 1971. Print.

*Cistercian Life*. Kalamazoo, MI: Cistercian Book Services, 1974. Print.

Merton, Thomas and Patrick Hart. *The Monastic Journey*. London, UK:
Sheldon Press, 1977. Print.

Merton, Thomas, Naomi Burton, and Patrick Hart. *Love and
Living*. Harcourt Brace Jovanovich, 1979. Print.

Merton, Thomas and Robert E. Daggy. *Introductions East and
West: The Foreign Prefaces of Thomas Merton*. Oakland, CA:
Unicorn Press, 1981. Print.

**Novels**

*My Argument with the Gestapo: A Macaronic Journal*. New York:
Doubleday, 1969. Print.

**Poetry**

*Thirty Poems*. Norfolk, CT: New Directions, 1944. Print.

*A Man in the Divided Sea*. Norfolk, CT: New Directions, 1946. Print.

*The Tears of the Blind Lions*. Norfolk, CT: New Directions, 1949. Print.

*The Strange Islands: Poems*. Norfolk, CT: New Directions, 1957. Print.

*Selected Poems*. Norfolk, CT: New Directions, 1959. Print.

*Emblems of a Season of Fury*. Norfolk, CT: New Directions. 1963. Print.

*On the Banks of Monks Pond*. Lexington, KY: U P of Kentucky, 1989. Print.

*Cables to the Ace*. Norfolk, CT: New Directions, 1968. Print.

*The Geography of Lograire*. Norfolk, CT: New Directions, 1969. Print.

*The Collected Poems of Thomas Merton*. Norfolk, CT: New Directions, 1977. Print.

*In The Dark Before Dawn: New Selected Poems of Thomas Merton*. Norfolk, CT: New Directions. 2005. Print.

**Social Issues/Essays**

*Seeds of Destruction*. New York: Farrar, Straus and Giroux. 1964. Print.

*Gandhi on Non-Violence*. Norfolk, CT: New Directions. 1965. Print.

*Faith and Violence*. Notre Dame, IN: University of Notre Dame P, 1968. Print.

*The Non-Violent Alternative*. New York: Farrar, Straus and Giroux, 1980. Print.

*The Hidden Ground of Love: Letters on Religious Experience and Social Concerns (Letters, 1)*. New York: Farrar, Straus, and Giroux, 1985. Print.

*Opening the Bible*. Minneapolis, MN: Fortress Press, 1986. Print.

*A Vow of Conversation: Journals 1964-1965*. New York: Farrar, Straus, and Giroux, 1988. Print.

*Thomas Merton in Alaska: The Alaskan Conferences, Journals and Letters*. New York: New Directions, 1988. Print.

*The Road to Joy: Letter to New and Old Friends (Letters, II)*. New York: Farrar, Straus, and Giroux, 1989. Print.

*The School of Charity: Letters on Religious Renewal and Spiritual Direction (Letters, III)*. New York: Farrar, Straus, and Giroux, 1990. Print.

*The Courage for Truth: Letters to Writers (Letters, IV)*. New York: Farrar, Straus, and Giroux, 1993. Print.

*Witness to Freedom: Letters in Times of Crisis (Letters, V)*. New York: Farrar, Straus, and Giroux, 1994. Print.

*Run to the Mountain: The Story of a Vocation (Journals, I: 1939-1941)*. San Francisco: Harper, 1995. Print.

*Entering the Silence: Becoming a Monk and Writer (Journals, II: 1941-1952)*. New York: HarperCollins, 1996. Print.

*A Search for Solitude: Pursuing the Monk's True Life (Journals, III: 1952-1960)*. San Francisco: Harper, 1996. Print.

*Turning Toward the World: The Pivotal Years (Journals, IV: 1960-1963)*. San Francisco: Harper, 1996. Print.

*Dancing in the Water of Life: Seeking Peace in the Hermitage (Journals, V: 1963- 1965)*. New York: HarperCollins, 1997. Print.

*Learning to Love: Exploring Solitude and Freedom (Journals VI: 1966-1967)*. San Francisco: Harper, 1997. Print.

*The Other Side of the Mountain: The End of the Journey (Journals VII: 1967-1968)*. New York: HarperOne, 1998. Print.

*The Intimate Merton: His Life from His Journals*. San Francisco, CA: HarperOne, 1999. Print.

*Dialogues with Silence*. New York: HarperOne, 2001. Print.

*Love and Living*. New York: Harcourt Trade Publishers, 2002. Print.

*The Inner Experience*. San Francisco: Harper, 2003. Print.

*Seeking Paradise: The Spirit of the Shakers*. Maryknoll, NY: Orbis Books, 2003. Print.

*Peace in a Post-Christian Era*. Maryknoll, NY: Orbis Books, 2004. Print.

# Jesse Stuart

## 1906-1984

Greenup County, Kentucky native Jesse Stuart was an accomplished poet, short story writer, novelist, and essayist by the time he was in his 40s. In 1934, he received the Jeannette Sewal Davis poetry prize for his first major book of poetry *Man with a Bull-Tongue Plow* (1934), which included 703 sonnets, many mimicking the style of great Scottish poet Robert Burns. The book was described by the Irish poet George William Russell as the greatest work of poetry to come out of America since Walt Whitman published *Leaves of Grass*. He was the recipient of many awards, among them a Guggenheim Fellowship (1937), the Academy of Arts and Sciences award, the Thomas Jefferson

Memorial award, the Berea College Centennial award for literature, the Academy of American Poets award, several honorary
degrees, and a nomination for the Pulitzer Prize for his 1975
poetry collection, *The World of Jesse Stuart*.

Stuart is known as one of the more remarkable and
original writers in American literature. He was extremely prolific,
publishing over 60 major works of children's books, juvenile
fiction, autobiography, biography, essays, history/sociology,
novels, short fiction, and poetry.

James Gifford, CEO & Senior Editor of the Jesse Stuart
Foundation, says that, "Jesse Stuart wrote furiously, like a man
killing snakes."

Critics were divided on their opinions of Stuart, many sug-
gesting that his writing was largely uneven. Others heaped great
praise on his work. Regardless, he consistently commanded a
broad popular audience. Because of the supposed uneven
quality of his writing and its apparent regional focus, he was often
maligned and sometimes ignored by the mainstream of literary
opinion. One of his trademarks in fiction was the claim that all
his stories were based on true stories that happened to himself
or to people he knew.

Born in a log cabin in W-Hollow in the hills of eastern
Kentucky, Stuart was the first in his family to finish high school,
graduating from Greenup High School in 1926. He worked his
way through Lincoln Memorial University, a small mountain
college in Tennessee, and graduated in 1929. While there, he
studied under novelist Harry Harrison Kroll, a well-known writer
of his day and one of Stuart's greatest influences. With Kroll's
encouragement, Stuart began writing poems, some of which
were published in the school newspaper. He was a classmate of

James Still, another highly regarded Kentucky writer.

After college, he returned to his native Eastern Kentucky to serve two years of public school teaching and administrative service (he twice served as principal of McKell High School in Greenup County—1933-1937 & 1956-1957). He then decided to enroll in graduate school at Vanderbilt University to pursue an M.A. in English. He chose Vanderbilt for its resident Fugitive-Agrarians, which included noted poets, writers, and teachers such as Donald Davidson, Robert Penn Warren, John Crowe Ransom, Alan Tate, Andrew Lytle, John Donald Wade, Clyde Curry, and Edwin Mims. An unfortunate fire in his dormitory destroyed the only copy of his thesis. This, coupled with a lack of adequate finances, prompted him to abandon graduate school and return to his homeland in eastern Kentucky.

He married Naomi Deane Norris in 1939 and they settled on his ancestral land in W-Hollow near Greenup, Kentucky. They had one daughter, Jessica Jane, who also became an accomplished novelist and poet. Stuart served as a Lieutenant (Junior Grade) in the United States Navy during World War II. He served as Kentucky's Poet Laureate from 1954-1955.

Stuart was widely traveled, having used his Guggenheim Fellowship to travel to Scotland. He served as visiting professor of English and education at the American University, Cairo, Egypt, during 1960 and 1961; in 1962 and 1963 he served as an American specialist abroad for the Bureau of Educational and Cultural Affairs of the State Department. He also served in the Middle and Far East as a lecturer for the United States Information Service. In the fall of 1962, he and his wife Deane left Greenup County for a five-month tour which included over 400 speaking engagements through Lebanon, Syria, Iraq, Iran, Egypt,

Afghanistan, East Pakistan, India, Thailand, the Philippines, Hong Kong, Taiwan, Japan, and Korea. All his life, Stuart was a tireless traveller and lecturer, rivalling Mark Twain in the scope of his travels.

Prior to his death on February 17, 1984, Stuart had been seriously ill and bedfast for four years, following a long history of heart attacks and a massive stroke. He is buried in the Plum Grove cemetery near his home in W-Hollow.

### Sources

Blair, Everetta Love. *Jesse Stuart: His Life and Works.* Columbia, SC: U of South Carolina P, 1967. Print.

Brosi, George and Jerry A. Herndon. *Jesse Stuart, The Man & His Books.* Ashland, KY: The Jesse Stuart Foundation, 1988. Print.

Clarke, Mary Washington. *Jesse Stuart's Kentucky.* New York: McGraw-Hill, 1968. Print.

Dick, David. *Jesse Stuart: The Heritage A Biography.* North Middletown, KY: Plum Lick Publishing, Inc., 2005. Print.

Foster, Ruel. *Jesse Stuart.* New York: Twayne Publishers, 1968. Print.

Gifford, James and Erin R. Kazee. *Jesse Stuart: An Extraordinary Life.* Ashland, KY: The Jesse Stuart Foundation, 2010. Print.

Herndon, Jerry A. "Jesse Hilton Stuart." *The Kentucky Encyclopedia.* Ed. John Kleber. Lexington, KY: U P of Kentucky, 1992. 858-859. Print.

"Jesse Stuart." *Kentucky in American Letters: Volume III 1913-1975.* Ed. Dorothy Edwards Townsend. Georgetown, KY: Georgetown College P, 1976. Print. 328-333.

"Jesse Stuart: A Man of the Country, a Man of the World." *Kentucky Monthly.* Online. Accessed 12 Aug., 2014. <http://www.kentuckymonthly.com/culture/people/jesse-stuart/>.

"Jesse Stuart Biography." *Enotes: Great Authors of World
    Literature, Critical Edition*. Online. Accessed 11 Aug. 2014.
    <http://www.enotes.com/topics/jesse-stuart>.
"Jesse Stuart: Split Cherry Tree." *Wordpress.com*. Online.
    Accessed 11 Aug. 2014.
    <http://ashley2121.wordpress.com/jesse-stuart-biography/>.
Pennington, Lee. *The Dark Hills of Jesse Stuart*. Cincinnati,
    OH: Harvest Press, 1967. Print.
Perry, Dick. *Reflections of Jesse Stuart*. New York: McGraw-
    Hill, 1971. Print.
Richardson, H. Edward. *Jesse: The Biography of an American
    Writer, Jesse Hilton Stuart*. New York: McGraw-Hill, 1984. Print.

## Selected Bibliography

### Autobiographical

*Beyond Dark Hills*, E.P. Dutton & Co., Inc., 1938. Print.
_____ (reprint). Ashland, KY: Jesse Stuart Foundation, 1996. Print.
*The Thread that Runs So True*. New York: Charles Scribner's
    Sons. 1949 . Print.
*The Year of My Rebirth*. New York: McGraw-Hill, 1956. Print.
_____ (reprint) Ashland, KY: Jesse Stuart Foundation, 1991. Print.
*To Teach, To Love*. New York: World Pub. Co., 1970. Print.
_____ (reprint). Ashland, KY: Jesse Stuart Foundation, 1987. Print.
*My World*. Lexington, KY: U P of Kentucky, 1975. Print.
*Dandelions on the Acropolis*. Danbury, CT: Archer Editions
    Press, 1978. Print.
*The Kingdom Within: A Spiritual Autobiography*. New York: McGraw-
    Hill, 1979. Print.

### Biography

*God's Oddling: The Story of Mick Stuart, My Father*. New York:
    McGraw-Hill, 1960. Print.

### Essays

*Lost Sandstones and Lonely Skies*. Danbury, CT: Archer Editions
    Press, 1979. Print.

*If I Were Seventeen Again: And Other Essays*. Danbury, CT: Archer Editions Press, 1980. Print.

**History/Sociology**

*Tennessee Hill Folk*. Nashville, TN: Vanderbilt University Press, 1972. Print.

*Up The Hollow from Lynchburg* (with Joe Clark). New York: McGraw-Hill, 1975. Print.

**Juvenile and Children's Books**

*The Beatinest Boy* Whittlesey House, 1953. Print.

\_\_\_\_\_ (reprint). Ashland, KY: Jesse Stuart Foundation, 1989. Print.

*A Penny's Worth of Character*. New York: McGraw-Hill/Whittlesey House, 1954. Print

\_\_\_\_\_ (reprint). Ashland, KY: Jesse Stuart Foundation, 1993. Print.

*Red Mule*. New York: McGraw-Hill, 1955. Print

\_\_\_\_\_ (reprint). Ashland, KY: Jesse Stuart Foundation, 1993. Print.

*The Rightful Owner*. New York: McGraw-Hill/Whittlesey House, 1960. Print.

*Andy Finds a Way*. New York: McGraw-Hill/Whittlesey House, 1961. Print.

*A Ride with Huey, the Engineer*. St. Helena, CA: James Beard, 1960. Print.

\_\_\_\_\_ (reprint). New York: McGraw-Hill, 1966. Print.

\_\_\_\_\_ (reprint). Ashland, KY: Jesse Stuart Foundation, 1988. Print.

*Old Ben*. New York: McGraw-Hill, 1970. Print.

\_\_\_\_\_ (reprint). Ashland, KY: Jesse Stuart Foundation, 1992. Print.

**Novels**

*Trees of Heaven*. New York: E.P. Dutton & Co., Inc. 1940 . Print.

\_\_\_\_\_ (reprint). Lexington, KY: U P of Kentucky, 1980. Print.

*Taps for Private Tussie*. New York: E.P. Dutton, 1943. Print.

*Mongrel Mettle: The Autobiography of a Dog*. New York: E.P. Dutton. 1944. Print.

*Foretaste of Glory*. New York: E. P. Dutton and Co., Inc., 1946. Print.

\_\_\_\_\_ (reprint). Lexington, KY: U P of Kentucky, 1986. Print.

*Hie to the Hunters*. New York: McGraw-Hill/Whittlesey House, 1950. Print.

\_\_\_\_\_ (reprint). Ashland, KY: Jesse Stuart Foundation, 1996. Print.

*The Good Spirit of Laurel Ridge*. New York: McGraw-Hill, 1953. Print.

*Daughter of the Legend*. New York: McGraw-Hill, 1965. Print.

\_\_\_\_\_ (reprint). Ashland, KY: The Jesse Stuart Foundation, 1994. Print.

*Mr. Gallion's School*. New York: McGraw-Hill, 1967. Print.

*The Land Beyond the River*. New York: McGraw-Hill, 1973. Print.

*Come to My Tomorrowland*. Nashville, TN: Aurora Publishers, Inc., 1971. Print.

*Cradle of the Copperheads*. New York: McGraw-Hill, 1988. Print.

**Poetry**

*Harvest of Youth*. Howe, OK: Scroll Press, 1930. Print.

\_\_\_\_\_ (reprint). Berea, KY: The Council of Southern Mountains, 1964. Print.

\_\_\_\_\_ (reprint). Ashland, KY: The Jesse Stuart Foundation, 1998. Print.

*Man with a Bull-Tongue Plow*. New York: E.P. Dutton & Co., Inc., 1934. Print.

*Album of Destiny*. New York: E. P. Dutton & Co., Inc., 1944. Print.

*Kentucky is My Land*. Ashland, KY: Economy Printers, 1952. Print.

\_\_\_\_\_ (reprint). Ashland, KY: The Jesse Stuart Foundation, 1987. Print.

*Hold April*. New York: McGraw-Hill, 1962. Print.

*Autumn Lovesong*. Kansas City, MO: Hallmark Editions, 1971. Print.

*The World of Jesse Stuart: Selected Poems*. Ed. J.R. LeMaster. New York: McGraw-Hill, 1975. Print.

*The Only Place We Live*. Ed. Mark E. Lefebvre. Madison, WI: Wisconsin House, 1976. Print.

*The Seasons of Jesse Stuart: An Autobiography in Poetry*. Ed. Wanda Hicks. Lynnville, TN: Archer Editions Press, 1976. Print.

*Land of Honey Colored Wind* (Poetry & Short Stories). Ed. Jerry
Herndon. Ashland, KY: The Jesse Stuart Foundation, 1981.
Print.

*Songs of a Mountain Plowman*. Ed. Jim Wayne Miller. Ashland, KY:
The Jesse Stuart Foundation, 1986. Print.

**Short Story Collections**

*Head o' W-Hollow*. New York: E. P. Dutton & Co., Inc., 1936.
Print.

*Tim: A Story.* Cincinnati, OH: Little Man Magazine, 1939. Print.

_____ (reprint). Cincinnati, OH: Harvest Press, 1968. Print.

*Men of the Mountains*. New York: E. P. Dutton & Co., Inc., 1941.
Print.

_____ (reprint). Lexington, KY: U P of Kentucky, 1979. Print.

*Tales from the Plum Grove Hills*. New York: E. P. Dutton & Co.,
Inc., 1946. Print.

_____ (reprint). Ashland, KY: Jesse Stuart Foundation, 1997. Print.

*Plowshare in Heaven*. New York: McGraw-Hill, 1958. Print.

*Save Every Lamb*. New York: McGraw-Hill, 1964. Print.

*My Land Has a Voice*. New York: McGraw-Hill, 1966. Print.

*Seven by Jesse*. Terre Haute, IN: Indiana Council of Teachers of
English, 1970. Print.

*A Jesse Stuart Harvest*. New York: Dell Publishing Co., 1965.
Print.

_____ (reprint). New York: Mockingbird/Ballantine Books (Random
House), 1974. Print.

*Stories by Jesse Stuart*. New York: McGraw-Hill, 1968. Print.

*Come Gentle Spring*. New York: McGraw-Hill. 1969. Print.

_____ (reprint). Ashland, KY: Jesse Stuart Foundation, 2008.
Print.

*Come Back to the Farm*. New York: McGraw-Hill, 1971. Print.

_____ (reprint). Ashland, KY: Jesse Stuart Foundation, 2001. Print.

*Dawn of the Remembered Spring*. New York: McGraw Hill, 1972. Print.

*32 Votes Before Breakfast*. New York: McGraw-Hill, 1974. Print.

*Land of Honey Colored Wind* (Poetry & Short Stories). Ed. Jerry
Herndon. Ashland, KY: The Jesse Stuart Foundation, 1981.
Print.

*The Best Loved Stories of Jesse Stuart*. Ed. Harold E.
Richardson. New York: McGraw-Hill, 1982. Print.

*Clearing in the Sky & Other Stories*. Lexington, KY: U P of
Kentucky, 1984. Print.

*New Harvest: Forgotten Stories of Kentucky's Jesse Stuart*. Ed.
David R. Palmore. Ashland, KY: The Jesse Stuart
Foundation, 2003. Print.

# CHAPTER THREE
## 2015

Photograph by James B. Goode.

# Wendell Berry

## 1934-

Wendell Berry is Kentucky's most prolific and well-known living writer. He has mastered three genres: fiction (both novels and short stories), poetry, and non-fiction. His book publications, to date, comprise 88 volumes published by a wide variety of publishers: Houghton Mifflin, Harcourt, Brace, Jovanovich, Pantheon, Orion, Avon Books, Shoemaker & Hoard, North Point, Counterpoint, Sierra Club, The University Press of Kentucky, Larkspur, Safe Harbor Books, Gnomon, Golgonooza Press, Sand Dollar, and others. Berry's writing and publishing career began with his first novel, *Nathan Coulter* (1960). His first book of poetry, *The Broken Ground*, was released in 1964 and his first book of non-fiction, *The Long-Legged* House, in 1969.

His writing is grounded in the notion that one's work ought to be rooted in and responsive to one's place. His philosophy of peace, environmentalism, conservation and regard for the Earth is best found in his own words:

> *But when nothing is valued for what it is, everything is destined to be wasted. Once the values of things refer only to their future usefulness, then an infinite withdrawal of value from the living present has begun. Nothing (and nobody) can then exist that is not theoretically replaceable by something (or somebody) more valuable. The country that we (or some of us) had thought to make our home becomes instead 'a nation rich in natural resources'; the good bounty of the land begins its mechanical metamorphosis into junk, garbage, silt, poison, and other forms of 'waste.' The inevitable result of such an economy is that no farm or any other usable property can safely be regarded by anyone as a home, no home is ultimately worthy of our loyalty, nothing is ultimately worth doing, and no place or task or person is worth a lifetime's devotion. 'Waste,' in such an economy, must eventually include several categories of humans—the unborn, the old, 'disinvested' farmers, the unemployed, the 'unemployable.' Indeed, once our homeland, our source, is regarded as a resource, we are all sliding downward toward the ashheap [sic] or the dump.*

Berry has deep roots in Kentucky, being the eldest of four children born to Virginia Erdman Berry and John Marshall Berry, a lawyer and tobacco farmer in Henry County. The families of both his parents have farmed in Henry County for at least five generations. In 1965, Berry moved to a farm he purchased at Lane's Landing in Henry County and began growing corn and small grains on what eventually became a 125-acre homestead. Berry has farmed, resided, and written at Lane's Landing to the present day. He has written about his early experiences on the land and about his decision to return to it in essays such as "The Long-Legged House" and "A Native Hill."

Berry attended secondary school at Millersburg Military Institute and earned a B.A. and M.A. in English at the University of Kentucky. Berry also attended Stanford University's creative writing program as a Wallace Stegner Fellow. He studied under Stegner in a seminar, with such notable classmates as Edward Abbey, Larry McMurtry, Robert Stone, Ernest Gaines, Tillie Olsen, and Ken Kesey.

From 1962 to 1964, he taught English at New York University's University College in the Bronx. He then taught creative writing at the University of Kentucky from 1964-1977. After a ten-year hiatus, he returned to the English Department of the University of Kentucky, where he taught from 1987-1993.

Early in his writing career, Berry was awarded a Guggenheim Foundation Fellowship (1961), *Poetry Magazine*'s Bess Hokin Prize (1967), Borestone Mountain Poetry Award (1969), National Institute of Arts and Letters Award for Excellence in Writing (1971), Friends for American Writers Award (1975), and the Lannan Foundation Award (1989).

In the 1990s, he was given the T. S. Eliot Award (1994),

The Orion Society John Hay Award (1993), *Sewanee Review* Aiken Taylor Award for Modern American Poetry (1994), and the Thomas Merton Award (1999).

Most recently, Berry was awarded the Poets' Prize (2000), Art of Fact Award for Non-Fiction (2006), The Cleanth Brooks Medal for Lifetime Achievement from the Fellowship of Southern Writers (2009), Fellowship of Southern Writers Award (2012), The National Humanities Medal (2012), Fellowship of The American Academy of Arts and Sciences (2013), and the 41st Jefferson Lecture in the Humanities (April 23, 2012).

Berry was bestowed The Roosevelt Institute's Freedom Medal (2013), The Richard C. Holbrooke Distinguished Achievement Award of the Dayton Literary Peace Prize (2013), and was elected a member of The American Academy of Arts and Sciences in Humanities and Arts (2013).

### Sources

Bittman, Mark. "Wendell Berry, American Hero." *The New York Times* 24 April 2012. Online. Accessed 12 Dec. 2014. <https://opinionator.blogs.nytimes.com/2012/04/24/wendell-berry-american-hero/?_r=0>.

McClanahan, Ed. "Wendell Erdman Berry" *The Kentucky Encyclopedia*. Ed. John Kleber. Lexington, Ky.: U P of Kentucky, 1992. 73-74. Print.

Skinner, David. "Wendell Berry Biography." *National Endowment for the Humanities*. Online. Accessed 12 Dec. 2014. <https://www.neh.gov/about/awards/jefferson-lecture/wendell-e-berry-biography>.

"Wendell Berry: Farmer, Ecologist, and Author." *The Mother Earth News*. March/April 1973. Online. Accessed 12 Dec. 2014. <http://www.motherearthnews.com/Nature-and-Environ-ment/wendell-berry>.

"Wendell Berry." *Kentucky in American Letters: Volume III 1913-1975*. Ed. Dorothy Edwards Townsend. Georgetown, KY: Georgetown College P, 1976. 33-35. Print.

"Wendell Berry." *Official Site*. Online. Accessed 12 Dec. 2014. <http://wendellberrybooks.com/>.

"Wendell Berry." *The Poetry Foundation*. Online. Accessed 12 Dec. 2014. <https://www.poetryfoundation.org/poems-and-poets/poets/detail/wendell-berry>.

## Selected Bibliography

**Fiction**

*Nathan Coulter*. Boston: Houghton Mifflin, 1960. Print.

*A Place on Earth*. Boston: Harcourt, Brace, 1967. Print.

*The Memory of Old Jack*. New York: Harcourt, Brace, Jovanovich 1974. Print.

*A Place on Earth*. San Francisco: North Point, 1983. Print.

*Nathan Coulter*. San Francisco: North Point, 1985. Print.

*The Wild Birds: Six Stories of the Port William Membership*. San Francisco: North Point, 1986. Print.

*Remembering*. San Francisco: North Point, 1988. Print.

*Fidelity: Five Stories*. New York: Pantheon, 1992. Print.

*Watch with Me and Six Other Stories of the Yet-Remembered Ptolemy Proudfoot and His Wife, Miss Minnie, Née Quinch*. New York: Pantheon, 1994. Print.

*A World Lost*. Washington, D.C.: Counterpoint, 1996. Print.

*Jayber Crow*. Washington, D.C.: Counterpoint, 2000. Print.

*A Place on Earth*. Washington, D.C.: Counterpoint, 2001. Print.

*The Memory of Old Jack*. Washington, D.C.: Counterpoint 2001. Print.

*Three Short Novels* (*Nathan Coulter, Remembering, A World Lost*). Washington, D.C.: Counterpoint, 2002. Print.

*Hannah Coulter*. Washington, D.C.: Shoemaker & Hoard. 2004. Print.

*That Distant Land: The Collected Stories*. Washington, D.C.: Shoemaker & Hoard, 2004. Print.

*Andy Catlett: Early Travels*. Washington, D. C.: Shoemaker & Hoard, 2006. Print.

*Whitefoot: A Story from the Center of the World*. Berkeley: Counterpoint. 2009. Print.

*A Place in Time: Twenty Stories of the Port William Membership*. Berkeley: Counterpoint, 2012. Print.

**Non-Fiction**

*The Long-Legged House*. New York: Harcourt, Brace, Jovanovich, 1969. Print.

*The Hidden Wound*. Boston: Houghton Mifflin, 1970. Print.

*The Unforeseen Wilderness: Kentucky's Red River Gorge* (Photographs by Ralph Eugene Meatyard). Lexington, KY: U P of Kentucky, 1971. Print.

*A Continuous Harmony: Essays Cultural & Agricultural*. New York: Harcourt, Brace, 1972. Print.

*The Unsettling of America: Culture and Agriculture*. San Francisco: Sierra Club, 1977. Print.

*The Unsettling of America: Culture and Agriculture*. New York: Avon Books, 1978. Print.

*The Gift of Good Land: Further Essays Cultural and Agricultural*. San Francisco: North Point, 1981. Print

*Recollected Essays: 1965–1980*. San Francisco: North Point, 1981. Print.

*Standing by Words*. San Francisco: North Point, 1983. Print.

*Meeting the Expectations of the Land: Essays in Sustainable Agriculture and Stewardship*. Eds. Wes Jackson and Bruce Colman. San Francisco: North Point, 1984. Print.

*The Unsettling of America: Culture and Agriculture*. San Francisco: Sierra Club, 1986. Print.

*Home Economics: Fourteen Essays*. San Francisco: North Point, 1987. Print.

*Descendants and Ancestors of Captain James W. Berry* (with Laura Berry). Bowling Green, KY: Hub, 1990. Print.

*Harlan Hubbard: Life and Work*. Lexington, KY: U P of Kentucky, 1990. Print.

*What Are People For?* New York: North Point, 1990. Print.

*Standing on Earth: (Selected Essays)*. U K: Golgonooza Press, 1991. Print.

*The Unforeseen Wilderness: Kentucky's Red River Gorge* (Photographs by Ralph Eugene Meatyard). San Francisco: North Point, 1991. Print.

*Sex, Economy, Freedom & Community*. New York: Pantheon, 1992. Print.

*Another Turn of the Crank*. Washington, D.C.: Counterpoint, 1996. Print.

*Grace: Photographs of Rural America* (with Gregory Spaid and Gene Logsdon). New London, New Hampshire: Safe Harbor Books, 2000. Print.

*Life Is a Miracle*. Washington, D.C.: Counterpoint, 2000. Print.

*In the Presence of Fear: Three Essays for a Changed World*. Great Barrington, MA: Orion, 2001. Print.

*The Art of the Commonplace: The Agrarian Essays of Wendell Berry*. Ed. Norman Wirzba. Washington, D.C.: Counterpoint, 2002. Print.

*Citizens Dissent: Security, Morality, and Leadership in an Age of Terror* (With David James Duncan and Foreword by Laurie Lane-Zucker) Great Barrington, MA: Orion, 2003. Print.

*Citizenship Papers*. Washington, D.C.: Shoemaker & Hoard, 2003. Print.

*Tobacco Harvest: An Elegy*. Photographs by James Baker Hall. Lexington, KY: U P of Kentucky, 2004. Print.

*The Long-Legged House*. Washington, D.C.: Shoemaker & Hoard, 2004. Print.

*A Continuous Harmony: Essays Cultural & Agricultural*. Washington, D.C.: Shoemaker & Hoard, 2004. Print.

*Blessed Are the Peacemakers: Christ's Teachings about Love, Compassion & Forgiveness*. Washington, D.C.: Shoemaker & Hoard, 2005. Print.

*The Way of Ignorance and Other Essays*. Washington, D.C.: Shoemaker & Hoard, 2005. Print.

*Standing by Words*. Washington, D.C.: Shoemaker & Hoard, 2005. Print.

*The Unforeseen Wilderness: Kentucky's Red River Gorge* (Photographs by Ralph Eugene Meatyard). Washington, D.C.: Shoemaker & Hoard, 2006. Print.

*Bringing It to the Table: On Farming and Food*. Berkeley: Counterpoint, 2009. Print.

*The Gift of Good Land: Further Essays Cultural and Agricultural*. San Francisco: Washington, D.C.: Counterpoint, 2009. Print.

*Home Economics: Fourteen Essays*. Berkeley: Counterpoint, 2009. Print.

*Imagination in Place*. Berkeley: Counterpoint, 2010. Print.

*What Matters? Economics for a Renewed Commonwealth*. Berkeley: Counterpoint, 2010. Print.

*The Poetry of William Carlos Williams of Rutherford*. Berkeley: Counterpoint, 2011. Print.

*It All Turns on Affection: The Jefferson Lecture and Other Essays*. Berkeley: Counterpoint, 2012. Print.

*Distant Neighbors: The Selected Letters of Wendell Berry and Gary Snyder*. Ed. Chad Wriglesworth. Berkeley: Counterpoint, 2014. Print.

**Poetry**

*The Broken Ground*. New York: Harcourt, Brace, 1964. Print.

*November twenty six nineteen hundred sixty-three*. New York: Braziller, 1964. Print.

*Openings*. New York: Harcourt, Brace, 1968. Print.

*Farming: A Hand Book*. New York: Harcourt, Brace, Jovanovich, 1970. Print.

*The Country of Marriage*. New York: Harcourt, Brace, Jovanovich, 1973. Print.

*An Eastward Look*. Berkeley: Sand Dollar, 1974. Print.

*Sayings and Doings*. Frankfort, KY: Gnomon, 1975. Print.

*Clearing*. New York: Harcourt, Brace, 1977. Print.

*A Part*. San Francisco: North Point, 1980. Print.

*The Wheel*. San Francisco: North Point, 1982. Print.

*The Collected Poems, 1957-1982*. San Francisco: North Point, 1985. Print.

*Sabbaths: Poems*. San Francisco: North Point, 1987. Print.

*Traveling at Home*. Lewisburg, PA: Bucknell UP of Appletree Alley, 1988. Print.

*Traveling at Home*. San Francisco: North Point, 1989. Print.

*Entries*. New York: Pantheon, 1994. Print.

*The Farm*. Monterey, KY: Larkspur, 1995. Print.

*Entries*. Washington, D.C.: Counterpoint, 1997. Print.

*A Timbered Choir: The Sabbath Poems 1979-1997*. Washington, D.C.: Counterpoint, 1998. Print.

*The Selected Poems of Wendell Berry*. Washington, D.C.: Counterpoint, 1999. Print.

*The Gift of Gravity, Selected: Poems, 1968-2000*. U K: Golgonooza Press, 2002. Print.

*Sabbaths 2002*. Monterey, KY: Larkspur, 2004. Print.

*Given: New Poems*. Washington D.C.: Shoemaker & Hoard. 2005. Print.

*Window Poems*. Washington, D.C.: Shoemaker & Hoard, 2007. Print.

*Sabbaths 2006*. Monterey, KY: Larkspur, 2008. Print.

*The Mad Farmer Poems*. Berkeley: Counterpoint, 2008. Print.

*Leavings*. Berkeley: Counterpoint, 2010. Print.

*Farming: A Hand Book*. Berkeley: Counterpoint, 2011. Print.

*New Collected Poems*. Berkeley: Counterpoint, 2012. Print.

*This Day: Sabbath Poems Collected and New 1979-2013*. Berkeley: Counterpoint, 2013. Print.

Photograph by Guy Mendes.

# Guy Davenport

## 1927-2005

*"Lives do not have plots, only biographies do."*
— Guy Davenport,
*The Hunter Gracchus: And Other Papers on Literature and Art*

University of Kentucky English Professor Guy Davenport claimed that writing fiction was just a hobby, but he published eight collections of short stories, won third prize in the O Henry Awards (1974), and was awarded the 1981 Morton Douwen Zabel award for fiction from the American Academy and Institute of Arts and Letters.

Hilton Kramer, in *The New York Times Book Review*, wrote of Davenport's conception of the short-story form:

*He has given it some of the intellectual density of the learned essay, some of the lyric concision of the modern poem—some of its difficulty, too—and a structure that often resembles a film documentary. The result is a tour de force that adds something new to the art of fiction.*

South Carolina native Davenport could well have been called the quintessential Renaissance man, but one that believed new ideas are not new—they have roots in the wellspring of the past. He was variously called a "postmodernist," and a "metamodernist." His notions ranged from the ancient to the present.

Davenport's writing is filled with allusion and often delivered in a difficult prose style. He was frequently accused of being obscure. He once told a *Paris Review* interviewer:

*I don't think I've ever consciously befuddled... I might be a better writer if I didn't tuck in things for the reader to find out... the stories can still be read; the idea is that a deeper reading will continually be rewarded—this is the standard by which obscurity can be judged.*

He was the recipient of the 1992 MacArthur "Genius" Fellowship, intended to be an "... investment in a person's originality, insight, and potential..." and awarded to those who "show exceptional merit and promise for continued and enhanced creative work." He has shared this honor with such celebrated writers as Kentuckian Robert Penn Warren, poet Adrienne Rich, writer and critic Susan Sontag, novelist Cormac McCarthy, and Highlander Center activist John Gaventa.

Davenport was educated at Duke University, Merton College, Oxford, and Harvard University. His career at the University of Kentucky spanned over twenty-eight years, where he taught in the English Department.

Davenport is credited with having published over 45 books of poetry, fiction, and essays. He contributed countless chapters, introductions, essays, commentary, and creative writing to numerous anthologies, magazines, and journals. His best-known work was his collection of essays, *The Geography of the Imagination* (1981).

Erik Reece, his former student and friend said of him: "He was an unqualified genius, so he talked over everybody's head, but in a way that made you want to get to where he was."

After retiring in 1992, he published three additional volumes of short stories and three collections of essays. Davenport died in 2005 and donated his remains to the University of Kentucky College of Medicine for Teaching and Research Body Bequeathal Program.

### Sources

Derickson, Ralph. "Retired Professor Guy Davenport Dies." *University of Kentucky Public Relations* 4 Jan. 2005. Online. Accessed 6 Dec. 2014. <http://www.uky.edu/PR/News/Archives/2005/Jan2005/050104 _guy_davenport.htm>.

Lehmann-Haupt, Christopher. "Guy Davenport Dies at 77; Prolific Author and Illustrator." *The New York Times* 7 Jan. 2005. Online. Accessed 6 Dec. 2014. <http://www.nytimes.com/2005/01/07/books/guy-davenport-dies-at-77-prolific-author-and-illustrator.html>.

Sullivan, John Jeremiah. "Guy Davenport, The Art of Fiction No. 174." *The Paris Review* 163 (Fall 2002). Online. Accessed 6 Dec. 2014. <https://www.theparisreview.org/interviews/355/guy-davenport-the-art-of-fiction-no-174-guy-davenport>.

Taylor, Richard. "Guy Mattison Davenport, Jr." *The Kentucky Encyclopedia*. Ed. John Kleber. Lexington, Ky.: U P of Kentucky, 1992. 253-254. Print.

Crane, Joan St., Guy Davenport, and Richard Noble. *Guy Davenport: A Descriptive Bibliography*. Haverford: PA.: Green Shade, 1996. Print.

## Selected Bibliography

### Commentary and Essays

*The Intelligence of Louis Agassiz*. Boston: Beacon Press, 1963. Print.

*Key-Indexed Study Guide to Homer's Iliad*. Philadelphia, PA: Educational Research Associates, 1967. Print.

*Key-Indexed Study Guide to Homer's Odyssey*. Philadelphia, PA: Educational Research Associates, 1967. Print.

*The Geography of the Imagination*: *Forty Essays*. San Francisco: North Point Press, 1981. Print.

*Cities on Hills*: *A Study of I-XXX of Ezra Pound's Cantos*. Ann Arbor, MI: UMI Research Press, 1983. Print.

*Charles Burchfield's Seasons*. Portland, OR.: Pomegranate Artbooks, 1994. Print.

*The Drawings of Paul Cadmus*. New York: Rizzoli Publishing, 1989. Print.

*Every Force Evolves a Form*: *Twenty Essays*. San Francisco: North Point Press, 1987. Print.

*A Balthus Notebook*. New York: The Ecco Press, 1989. Print.

*The Hunter Gracchus and Other Papers on Literature and Art*. Berkley, CA.: Counterpoint, 1996. Print.

### Fiction

*Tatlin!*: *Six Stories* ( illustrated by Davenport). New York: Charles Scribner & Sons, 1974. Print.

*Da Vinci's Bicycle*: *Ten Stories* (illustrated by
Davenport). Baltimore: Johns Hopkins University Press,
1979. Print.

*Eclogues*: *Eight Stories* (illustrated by Roy Behrens). Baltimore:
Johns Hopkins University Press, 1981. Print.

*Apples and Pears and Other Stories* (illustrated by Davenport).
San Francisco: North Point Press, 1984. Print.

*The Jules Verne Steam Balloon*: *Nine Stories*. Baltimore: North
Point Press, 1987. Print.

*The Drummer of the Eleventh North Devonshire Fusiliers*.
Baltimore: North Point Press, 1990. Print.

*The Lark* (illustrated by Davenport). New York: Dim Gray Bar
Press, 1993. Print.

*A Table of Green Fields*: *Ten Stories*. New York: New Directions,
1993. Print.

*The Cardiff Team*: *Ten Stories*. New York: New Directions, 1996. Print.

*Twelve Stories*. Berkley, CA.: Counterpoint, 1997. Print.

*The Death of Picasso: New and Selected Writing*. Washington,
D.C.: Shoemaker and Hoard, 2003. Print.

*Wo es war, soll ich werden*: *The Restored Original Text*.
Champaign, IL: Finial Press, 2004. Print.

**Letters**

*A Garden Carried in a Pocket*: *Letters 1964–1968: Selected
Correspondence with Jonathan Williams*. Ed. Thomas
Meyer. Salisbury, CT: Green Shade, 2004. Print.

*Fragments from a Correspondence*. Ed. Nicholas Kilmer. *Arion: A
Journal of Humanities and Classics at Boston University*.
Winter 2006. 89-129. Print.

*Selected Letters: Guy Davenport and James Laughlin*. Ed. W. C.
Bamberger. New York: W. W. Norton & Co., 2007. Print.

*Objects on a Table*: *Harmonious Disarray in Art and Literature*.
Berkley, CA: Counterpoint, 1998. Print.

**Paintings and Drawings**

*A Balance of Quinces*: *The Paintings and Drawings of Guy Davenport, with an essay by Erik Anderson Reece*. New York: New Directions, 1996. Print.

*50 Drawings*. New York: Dim Gray Bar Press, 1996. Print.

*The Counterfeiters: An Historical Comedy* (includes Davenport's crosshatched crow quill and ink work, 10 full-page drawings). Champaign, IL: Dalkey Archive Press, 2005. Print.

*The Stoic Comedians: Flaubert, Joyce, Beckett Comedians* (includes Davenport's crosshatched crow quill and ink work, 10 full-page drawings). Berkeley, CA: U of California P, 1974. Print.

**Poetry**

*Cydonia Florentia*. Cambridge, MA: The Lowell-Adams House Printers/Laurence Scott, 1966. Print.

*Flowers and Leaves*: *Poema vel Sonata, Carmina Autumni Primaeque Veris Transformationem* (illustrated by Davenport). New York: W.W. Norton & Co., Inc./Bamberger Books, 1991. Print.

*The Resurrection in Cookham Churchyard*. New York: Jordan Davies, 1982. Print.

*Goldfinch Thistle Star* (illustrated by Lachlan Stewart). New York: Red Ozier Press, 1983. Print.

*Thasos and Ohio*: *Poems and Translations, 1950-1980*. San Francisco: North Point Press, 1986. Print.

**Translations**

*Carmina Archilochi*: *The Fragments of Archilochos*. Oakland, CA: University of California Press, 1964. Print.

*Sappho*: *Songs and Fragments*. Ann Arbor, MI: U of Michigan P, 1965. Print.

*Herakleitos and Diogenes*. San Francisco: Grey Fox Press, 1979. Print.

*The Mimes of Herondas*. San Francisco: Grey Fox Press, 1981. Print.

*Maxims of the Ancient Egyptians* (from Boris de Rachewiltz's Massime
degli antichi egiziani, 1954). Parkstone, Poole, Dorset,
UK: The Pace Trust, 1983. Print.

*Anakreon*. Tuscaloosa, Al: The University of Alabama/Parallel
Editions, 1991. Print.

*Archilochos, Sappho, Alkman: Three Lyric Poets*. Oakland, CA:
U of California P, 1980. Print.

*The Logia of Yeshua: The Sayings of Jesus* (with Benjamin
Urrutia). Berkley, CA: Counterpoint, 1996. Print.

*Greeks*. New York: New Directions, 1995. Print.

# Elizabeth Hardwick

## 1916-2007

When Elizabeth Hardwick died at the age of 91 in 2007, *The New York Times* described her as a critic, essayist, fiction writer, and co-founder of the *New York Review of Books* and one who "... went from being a studious southern belle to a glittering member of the New York City intellectual elite." This was an obvious reference to her having been born in Lexington, Kentucky, and educated in the public schools there (Lexington Junior High School and Henry Clay High School) and at The University of Kentucky where she earned a bachelor's degree (1938) and a master's degree (1939).

Interestingly, she turned down a fellowship in a doctoral

program at Louisiana State University, home of the *Southern Review* and a hotbed of southern literature, choosing instead to seek the Bohemian lifestyle associated with Columbia University in New York City while pursuing her doctoral degree in 17th Century English Literature. Because of the rarity of female faculty appointments in academia, she abandoned her pursuit in 1941 and returned to Kentucky to publish short stories, and write her first novel *The Ghostly Lover* (1945).

Her *New York Times* obituary recounts an interview conducted in 1979: "My aim was to be a New York Jewish Intellectual. I say 'Jewish' because of their tradition of rational skepticism; and also a certain deracination appeals to me—and their openness to European culture."

At age 32, Hardwick met poet Robert Lowell in early 1949 during a retreat at Yaddo, the artists' colony in Saratoga Springs. Despite Lowell's reputation as a tempestuous philanderer, she married him in July 1949, remaining married until their divorce in 1972. Their daughter Harriet was born in 1957.

Hilton Als, in his article "A Singular Woman," appearing in the July 13, 1998 issue of *The New Yorker*, described Hardwick as:

> *... a beautiful, ambitious girl from a large Protestant family in Lexington, Kentucky... [who] made a career of exploring the margins: furtive trips to evangelical tent meetings when she was a teenager, a stint as a Communist at the University of Kentucky, a mariage blanc to a gay man in New York, forays into the world of Negro jazz music, and marriage to a manic-depressive poet.*

Hardwick, Susan Sontag, Mary McCarthy, and Robert Lowell were involved in the founding of the *New York Review of Books* in 1963. She contributed more than one hundred reviews, articles, reflections, and letters to the magazine.

American novelist, Diane Johnson said that Hardwick was "part of the first generation of women intellectuals to make a mark in New York's literary circle." Joan Didion wrote of Hardwick, "Perhaps no one has written more poignantly about the ways in which women compensate for their relative physiological inferiority."

Scholar Lisa Levy said of her literary criticism:

*Her criticism often identified with mad or tortured women, what Didion identified as 'women adrift': Dorothy Wordsworth, Charlotte Brontë, Samuel Richardson's Pamela, Zelda Fitzgerald—rather than madmen and the women who loved them... She was conscious of the world, literary and lived, as comprising men, women, and their intersections, both rough and gentle.*

Hardwick was awarded a Guggenheim Fellowship in 1947 and received a Gold Medal from the American Academy of Arts and Letters in 1996; she was the author of three novels, a biography of Herman Melville, and four collections of essays.

Acclaimed novelist and essayist, Susan Sontag offered a poignant compliment about her writing, "Her sentences are burned in my brain. I think she writes the most beautiful sentences, more beautiful sentences than any living American writer."

Elizabeth Hardwick died in December 2, 2007 in Manhattan, New York.

## Sources

Als, Hilton. "A Singular Woman." *The New Yorker.* 13 July
    1998. Online. Accessed 12 Dec. 2014.
    <http://www.newyorker.com/magazine/1998/07/13/a-singular-
    woman>.

Bailey, Paul. "Elizabeth Hardwick: Writer, co-founder of 'The
    New York Review of Books' and long-suffering wife of Robert
    Lowell." *The Independent.* 8 Dec. 2007. Print.

Bradbury, Malcolm. "Elizabeth Hardwick in conversation."
    ICA Video (Trilion); Northbrook, IL: Anthony Roland Collection
    of Film on Art, 1986. Video Recording.

"Elizabeth Hardwick." *Kentucky in American Letters: Volume III
    1913-1975.* Ed. Dorothy Edwards Townsend. Georgetown, KY:
    Georgetown College P, 1976. 159-160. Print.

Lehmann-Haupt, Christopher. "Elizabeth Hardwick, Writer, Dies at
    91." *New York Times Obituary.* 4 Dec. 2007. Print.

Levy, Lisa. "An Original Adventure: The Life of Elizabeth
    Hardwick." *The Believer.* May 2008. Online. Accessed 12 Dec.
    2014. <http://www.believermag.com/issues/200805/?
    read=article_levy>.

O'Keeffe, Anthony. "Elizabeth Hardwick." *The Kentucky
    Encyclopedia.* Ed. John Kleber. Lexington, Ky.:
    U P of Kentucky, 1992. 405-406. Print.

Pickney, Darryl. "Elizabeth Hardwick, The Art of Fiction No. 87".
    *The Paris Review.* Summer 1985. Print.

## Selected Bibliography

**Biography:**

*Herman Melville.* New York: Penguin, 2000. Print.

**Criticism:**

*A View of My Own.* New York: Farr, Straus and Cudahy, 1962. Print.

*Seduction and Betrayal.* New York: Random House, 1974. Print.

*Bartleby in Manhattan* New York: Random House, 1983. Print.

*Sight-Readings: American Fictions.* New York: Random House, 1998.
    Print.

**Edited Collections**

*The Selected Letters of William James*. Ed. Elizabeth Hardwick.
New York: Doubleday, 1961. Print.

*Best American Essays*. Ed. Elizabeth Hardwick. New York: Houghton
Mifflin, 1986. Print.

**Essay (Magazine)**

"Reflections on Simone Weil." *Signs: Journal of Women in Culture
and Society* 1:1 (Autumn 1975), 83-91. Print.

**Novels**

*The Ghostly Lover*. New York: Harcourt, Brace, & Co., 1945. Print.

*The Simple Truth*. London: Weidenfeld & Nicolson, 1955. Print.

*Sleepless Nights*. New York: Random House, 1979. Print.

**Short Fiction Collection**

*The New York Stories of Elizabeth Hardwick*. New York: The New
York Review of Books, Inc., 2010. Print.

**Short Fiction (Magazine):**

"Evenings at Home." *Partisan Review*. April 1948. Print.

"A Florentine Conference." *Partisan Review* 18:3 (May-June 1951),
304-306. Print.

**Textbook:**

*Topics with Targets* (with Barbara Moore). Harmor Books, 1991. Print.

# Jim Wayne Miller

## 1936-1996

Jim Wayne Miller's primary tenet was to provide the reader with an environment of deep discovery. He said he was often amused when a tourist fisherman stepped into the clear water of his native Buncombe County North Carolina and discovered, much to his surprise, the pool was vastly deeper than he had imagined. "I want writing to be so transparent that the reader forgets he is reading and aware only that he is having an experience. He is suddenly plunged deeper than he expected and comes up shivering."

Miller was born in 1936 at Leicester, North Carolina on a seventy-acre farm. He was reared in a family of five younger

brothers and sisters. He left for Berea College in 1954 and grad-
uated with a Bachelor's Degree in Journalism (1958). He married
Mary Ellen Yates and they moved to Nashville, Tennessee; where
he earned his Ph.D. in German Language and Literature from
Vanderbilt University (1965). He studied under Fugitive poet
Donald Davidson and Hawthorne scholar Randall Stewart Miller.

While in Nashville, Miller wrote his seminal book of poetry
*Copperhead Cane*. After graduation, he and Mary Ellen settled
at Western Kentucky State University in Bowling Green where
he had a 33-year teaching career in the Department of Modern
Languages and Intercultural Studies. But he never strayed far
from his Appalachian roots, becoming one of the premier
Appalachian writers of his generation. He tirelessly promoted
writing among eager audiences who attended his numerous
workshops and speaking appearances throughout the South.

Appalachian scholar George Brosi said of Miller:

*... [he] lived life intensely. He drank prodigious*
*amounts of coffee and smoked many cigarettes*
*throughout every day and liked a good bourbon*
*during his long nights. When talking to either an*
*individual or a group, he listened intently and*
*responded enthusiastically. He carried his erudi-*
*tion perhaps more gracefully than anyone I've*
*ever met—never intruding upon a conversation in*
*a showy way, and typically seeking out ways to*
*learn from those who so often eagerly gathered*
*around him. I don't recall Jim Wayne Miller ever*
*leaving a conversation to go to bed.*

His most important books of poetry include: *Copperhead Cane*

(1964), *The More Things Change, The More They Stay the Same* (1971), *Dialogue With a Dead Man* (1974), *The Mountains Have Come Closer* (1980), *Vein of Words* (1984), *Nostalgia for 70* (1986), *Brier: His Book* (1988), and *The Brier Poems* (1997). His published novels include *Newfound* (1989) and *His First, Best Country* (1993).

He was awarded the Alice Lloyd Memorial Prize for Appalachian Poetry (1967), Thomas Wolfe Literary Award (1980), Zoe Kincaid Brockman Memorial Award, Appalachian Writers Association Book of the Year Award and Appalachian Consortium Laurel Leaves Award.

The Appalachian writers' community lost a great poet, novelist, essayist, and dedicated promoter of the literary arts when Jim Wayne Miller died at his home in Bowling Green, Kentucky August 18, 1996. George Brosi, Editor Emeritus of *Appalachian Heritage Magazine* said of Miller: "[He] is quite simply an icon in the field of Appalachian Literature—one of its earliest and most ardent supporters. Fred Chappell has commented that 'if it were not for Miller, the Appal-lit movement might have foundered before it got started.'"

Miller died August 18, 1996 at his home in Bowling Green.

### Sources

Ahrens, Sylvia. "Jim Wayne Miller: Universal Regionalist." *Kentucky English Bulletin* 47:2 (Winter 1998). 75-84. Print.

Arnold, Edwin T. and J.W. Williamson. "An Interview with Jim Wayne Miller." *Appalachian Journal* 6.3 (Spring 1979): 207-225. Print.

Baldwin, Thomas. "A Simple, Sophisticated Man." *Appalachian Heritage* 25:4 (Fall 1997). 8-13. Print.

Beattie, L. Elisabeth. "Jim Wayne Miller." *In Conversations with Kentucky Writers*. Ed. L. Elisabeth Beattie. Lexington, KY: U P of Kentucky, 1996. 242-261. Print.

Boone, Joy Bale. "Jim Wayne Miller." *The Kentucky Encyclopedia.*
Ed. John Kleber. Lexington, KY: U P of Kentucky, 1992. 637-
638. Print.

Brosi, George. "Jim Wayne Miller." *Appalachian Heritage* 37:3.
11-15. Print.

Caskey, Jefferson D. "The Writings of Jim Wayne Miller: A
Selective Bibliography." *Iron Mountain Review* 4:2 (Spring
1988). 37-40. Print.

Crooke, Jeff. "Sonnet Forms and Ballad Feelings." *Iron Mountain
Review* 4:2 (Spring 1988). 23. Print.

Crowe, Thomas Rain. "Rocks in the Stream: A Conversation with
Jim Wayne Miller." *Arts Journal* 14:11 (August 1989). 10-13.
Print.

Dyer, Joyce. "Accepting Things Near: Bibliography of Non-
Fiction by Jim Wayne Miller." *Appalachian Journal* 30:1 (Fall
2002). 64-73. Print.

_____. "The Brier Goes to College." *Appalachian Journal*
16:3 (Spring 1989). 112-113. Print.

_____. "Dialogue with a Dead Man." *Appalachian Journal*. 26:1
(Fall 1998). 32-43. Print.

_____. "Jim Wayne Miller." *Contemporary Poets, Dramatists,
Essayists, and Novelists of the South: A Bio-Bibliographical
Sourcebook.* Eds. Robert Bain and Joseph M. Flora.
Westport, CT: Greenwood, 1994. 344-359. Print.

Edwards, Grace Toney. "Holding the Mirror for Appalachia." *Iron
Mountain Review* 4:2 (Spring 1988). 24-28. Print.

Farrell, David. "Jim Wayne Miller." Video interview in Kentucky
Writers Oral History Project, University of Kentucky. Produced
and directed by Andy Spears, 1981. Film.

Grubbs, Morris A. "Jim Wayne Miller." *American Writers: A
Collection of Literary Biographies Supplement XX.* Ed. Jay
Parini. Detroit: Gale Cengage Learning, 2010. 161-176. Print.

Hall, Wade. "Jim Wayne Miller's Brier Poems: The Appalachian in
Exile." *Iron Mountain Review* 4:2 (Spring 1988). 29-33. Print.

"Jim Wayne Miller (1936-1996)." *Chapter 16.* 30 December
    2011. Online. Accessed 8 Dec. 2014.
    <http://www.chapter16.org/content/%5Bfield_revsubtitle-
    raw%5D-13>.

"Jim Wayne Miller." *Kentucky in American Letters: Volume III
    1913-1975.* Ed. Dorothy Edwards Townsend. Georgetown,
    KY: Georgetown College P, 1976. 234-237. Print.

Johnson, Don. "The Appalachian Homeplace: The Oneiric House in
    Jim Wayne Miller's 'The Mountains Have Come Closer.'" *Iron
    Mountain Review* 4:2 (Spring 1988). 34-36. Print.

Jones, Loyal. "An Interview: In Quest of the Briar." *Iron
    Mountain Review* 4:2 (Spring 1988) 13-21. Reprinted in
    *Appalachian and Beyond: Conversations with Writers from
    the Mountain South.* Ed. John Lang. Knoxville: U of Ten-
    nessee P, 2006. 53-72. Print.

_____. "Leicester Luminist Lighted Local Language and
    Lore." *Appalachian Heritage* 37:3 (Summer 2009): 27-34.
    Print.

Kelly, Patricia P. "An Interview with Jim Wayne Miller."
    *Journal of Reading* 34:8 (May 1991). 666-669. Print.

Kendrick, Leatha. "Hindman Writers' Workshop: Confirming a
    Community." *Appalachian Heritage* 25:4 (Fall 1997). 18-23. Print.

Kumin, Maxine. "The Poetry Workshop." *The Writer* (July 1963).
    Reprinted as "A Variegated Thread. *Iron Mountain Review* 4:2
    (Spring 1988). 22. Print.

Lang, John. "Jim Wayne Miller and the Brier's Cosmopolitan
    Regionalism." *Six Poets from the Mountain South.* Baton
    Rouge: Louisiana State U P, 2010. 3-37. Print.

Larson, Ron. "The Appalachian Personality. Interviews with
    Loyal Jones and Jim Wayne Miller." *Appalachian Heritage*
    11:3 (Summer 1983). 48-54. Print.

Lasater, Michael. *I Have a Place: The Poetry of Jim Wayne
    Miller.* Television profile. A production of Western Kentucky
    University Television Center (Bowling Green, Ky., 1985). Film.

Miller, Mary Ellen. "The Literary Influences of Jim Wayne
       Miller." *Appalachian Heritage* 37:3 (Summer 2009). 19-24.
       Print.

_____. "My Husband." *Appalachian Heritage* 25:4 (Fall 1997). 4-5.
       Print.

Miller, Ruth. "My Father." *Appalachian Heritage* (Fall 1997). 6-7. Print.

Minick, Jim. "Brier Visions': What Did He See?" *Journal of
       Kentucky Studies* 22 (2005). 135-138. Print.

Morgan, Robert. "Clearing Newground." *Appalachian Heritage* 25:4
       (Fall 1997). 24-30. Print.

Pendarvis, Edwina. "Sanctifying the Profane: Jim Wayne Miller's
       'Dialogue with a Dead Man.'" *Journal of Kentucky Studies* 22
       (2005). 139-143. Print.

Worthington, Marianne. "Lost in the American Funhouse': Magical
       Realism and Transfiguration in Jim Wayne Miller's *The Moun-
       tains Have Come Closer.*" *Journal of Kentucky Studies* 22
       (2005). 144-151. Print.

## Selected Bibliography
### Criticism & Translations

*The Figure of Fulfillment: Translations of the Poetry of Emil
       Lerperger.* Owensboro, KY: Green River Press, 1975. Print.

### Edited Works

*I Have a Place.* Pippa Passes, KY: Appalachian Center, Alice
       Lloyd College, 1981. Print.

*Songs of a Mountain Plowman.* By Jesse Stuart, with an
       introduction by Jim Wayne Miller. Morehead State University's
       Appalachian Development Center, 1986. Print.

_____ (reprint) Ashland, KY: Jesse Stuart Foundation, 1987. Print.

*The Wolfpen Poems.* By James Still, with an introduction by Jim
       Wayne Miller. Berea, KY: Berea College Press, 1986. Print.

*Kentucky is My Land.* By Jesse Stuart, with an afterword by Jim
       Wayne Miller. Ashland, KY: Jesse Stuart Foundation, 1987.
       Print.

*To Teach, To Love.* By Jesse Stuart, edited for re-issue by Jim Wayne Miller. Ashland, KY: Jesse Stuart Foundation, 1988. Print.

*A Ride with Huey the Engineer: Fact and Fiction from a colorful Era of America's Past.* By Jesse Stuart, edited for re-issue by Jim Wayne Miller. Ashland, KY: Jesse Stuart Foundation, 1988. Print.

*Jesse Stuart: The Man and His Books.* Eds. Jerry A. Herndon and George Brosi (with James M. Gifford and Jim Wayne Miller). Ashland, KY: Jesse Stuart Foundation, 1988. Print.

*A Penny's Worth of Character.* By Jesse Stuart, edited for re-issue by Jim Wayne Miller. Ashland, KY: Jesse Stuart Foundation, 1988. Print.

*A Jesse Stuart Reader.* Edited for re-issue by Jim Wayne Miller. Ashland, KY: Jesse Stuart Foundation, 1988. Print.

*Hie To the Hunters.* By Jesse Stuart, edited for re-issue by Jim Wayne Miller. Ashland, KY: Jesse Stuart Foundation, 1988. Print.

*The Beatinest Boy.* By Jesse Stuart, edited for re-issue by Jim Wayne Miller and Jerry Herndon. Ashland, KY: Jesse Stuart Foundation, 1989. Print.

*The Rightful Owner.* By Jesse Stuart, edited for re-issue by Jim Wayne Miller, James Gifford and Jerry Herndon. Ashland, KY: Jesse Stuart Foundation, 1989. Print.

**Essays**

*Sideswipes.* Big Timber, MT: Seven Buffaloes Press, 1986. Print.

*Round and Round with Kahlil Gibran* (with an introduction by Sharyn McCrumb). Blacksburg, VA: Rowan Mountain Press, 1990. Print.

**Novels**

*Newfound.* New York: Orchard Books, 1989. Print.

\_\_\_\_\_ (reprint). Frankfort, KY: Gnomon Press, 1996. Print.

**Poetry:**

*Copperhead Cane.* Nashville: Robert Moore Allen, 1964. Print.

_____ (reprinted as bilingual English-German, translated by
     Thomas Dorsett). Louisville: Grex Press Library Poetry
     Series, 1995. Print.

*The More Things Change the More They Stay the Same (*with art by
     Jill Baker). Frankfort, KY: Whippoorwill Press, 1971. Print.

*Dialogue With A Dead Man.* Athens: University of Georgia
     Press, 1974.

_____ (reprint). University Center, MI: Green River Press, 1978. Print.

*The Mountains Have Come Closer.* Boone, NC: Appalachian
     Consortium Press, 1980. Print.

*Vein of Words.* Big Timber, MT: Seven Buffaloes Press, 1984. Print.

*Nostalgia for 70.* Big Timber, MT: Seven Buffaloes Press,
     1986. Print.

*Brier, His Book.* Frankfort, KY: Gnomon Press, 1988. Print.

*The Wisdom of Folk Metaphor: The Brier Conducts a Laboratory
     Experiment.* Big Timber, MT: Seven Buffaloes Press, 1988.
     Print.

*The Brier Poems.* Ed. Johnathan Green. Frankfort, KY: Gnomon
     Press, 1997. Print.

*The Examined Life: Family, Community, and Work in American
     Literature.* Boone, NC: Appalachian Consortium Press, 1989.
     Print.

**Short Fiction:**

*His First, Best Country.* Frankfort, KY: Gnomon Press, 1987.

_____ (reprint). Frankfort, KY: Gnomon Press, 1993. Print.

**Textbooks & Guides:**

*Reading, Writing, Region: A Checklist, Purchase Guide and
     Directory for School and Community Libraries in Appalachia.*
     Boone, NC: Appalachian Consortium Press, 1984. Print.

# Effie Waller Smith

## 1879-1960

Because of the difficulties African American women faced in the post-Civil War era, Effie Waller Smith was an unlikely candidate to become one of the best-known poets of the early 1900s. She was born June 1, 1879 to former slaves Frank Waller and Alvindia "Sibbie" Ratliff on Chole Creek near Pikeville, Kentucky. Frank had been educated on the same Virginia plantation as Junte Kinte. Later, he became an aide to Stonewall Jackson and purportedly served Jackson his last meal. Frank Waller migrated to Pike County after the Civil War ended. Effie and her siblings Alfred and Rosa attended school through the eighth grade, and then she departed for Frankfort, Kentucky where she was trained as a teacher at The Kentucky Normal

School for Colored Persons (1900-1902). After her graduation, she held teaching posts in Kentucky and Tennessee for the next twelve years.

By 1902, Waller had published poetry in several local newspapers. She vanity published her first volume of poetry containing 110 poems titled, *Songs of the Months* (1904). This book was organized by sections, featuring one for each month of the year. The verses included love, patriotic, and nature themes. In 1909, two more volumes of her verse appeared. The first, *Rhymes from the Cumberland*, offers meditations and remembrances of the Kentucky-Virginia Cumberland Mountains area and musings on religion and romance.

In the second volume, *Rosemary and Pansies,* the verses focused on situational life issues. David Deskins, Waller's biographer, says that many of the poems in this volume "...are somber and subdued yet definite and conclusive as they examine issues and situations in life. There is a mood maintained throughout that sometimes delves into the mystical." During the early 1900s, Waller published three short stories in *Putnam's Monthly*: "The Tempting of Peter Stiles," "A Son of Sorrow," and "The Judgment of Roxenie."

Waller was only thirty-eight when her last published poem, "Autumn Wind" (a sonnet), appeared in the September 1917 issue of *Harper's Monthly*. For some unknown reason, she never published again. She lived the rest of her life in Wisconsin, where she had relocated in 1918, rearing an adopted daughter named Ruth Virginia Ratliff Smith, the daughter of deceased friend Polly Mullins Ratliff. Effie died in 1960 and is buried in Oak Hill Cemetery at Neenah, Wisconsin.

## Sources

Deskins, David. "Effie Waller Smith." *The Kentucky Encyclopedia*.
	Ed. John Kleber. Lexington, KY: U P of Kentucky, 1992. 829. Print.
_____. "Introduction to *The Collected Works of Effie Waller
	Smith*." Schomburg Library of Nineteenth-Century Black
	Women Writers. New York: Oxford University P, 1991. 6-7. Print.
_____. "Effie Waller Smith: An Echo Within the Hills." *Kentucky
	Review* 8 (Autumn 1988). 26-46. Print.
"Effie *Waller* Smith." *Find A Grave*. Online. Accessed 10 Dec. 2014.
	<http://www.findagrave.com/cgi-
	bin/fg.cgi?page=gr&GRid=6666592>.
"Effie Waller Smith." *PoemHunter.com*. Online. Accessed 10 Dec. 2014.
	<http://www.poemhunter.com/effie-waller-smith/biography>.
Engelhardt, Elizabeth. "Effie Waller Smith: African-American
	Appalachian Poetry from the Breaks." *Project Muse*. Online.
	Accessed 10 Dec. 2014.
	<https://muse.jhu.edu/article/250435>.
Hintz, Stephen C. "The Odyssey of Ruth Smith. *WELS Historical
	Institute Journal* 7 1:3 (1989). 11-13. Print.
Wollangk, JoEllen. "Effie Waller Smith is most unlikely 'Neenah
	Notable.'" Online. Accessed 10 Dec. 2014.
	<https://static1.squarespace.com/static/576b4c07cd0f68b308
	12e2e6/t/57bde38b5016e12b3dbdace8/1472062349368/
	EffieWallerSmith.pdf>.

## Selected Bibliography

### Collected Works

Smith, Effie Waller (with an introduction by David
	Deskins). *The Collected Works of Effie Waller Smith*.
	Ed. Henry Louis Gates, Jr. New York: Oxford University
	Press, 1991. Print.

### Poetry

*Songs of the Months*. New York: Broadway Publishing Company,
	1904. Print.

*Rhymes from the Cumberland.* New York: Broadway Publishing Company, 1909. Print.

*Rosemary and Pansies.* Boston: Richard G Badger: The Gorham Press, 1909. Print.

**Biographical**

Fraley, Jay. *Pike County News* 2 Apr. 1926. n.p. Print.

Kinder, Alice. *Appalachian News Express* 1980. n.p. Print.

Miller, James Wayne. *Open Eye* Spring 1989. n.p. Print.

**Poetry in Magazines & Journals**

"Autumn Winds." *Harper's* Sept. 1917. n.p. Print.

"Benignant Death." *Putman's Monthly and The Reader* Dec. 1908. n.p. Print.

"The Faded Blossoms." *The Independent* 20 July 1911. n.p. Print.

"The Shepherds' Vision." *The Independent* 24 December 1908. n.p. Print.

**Short Fiction**

"The Tempting of Peter Stiles." *Putnam's Monthly* Feb. 1908. 597-602. Print.

"A Son of Sorrow." *Putnam's Monthly* Dec. 1908. 274-280. Print.

"The Judgment of Roxenie." *Putnam's Monthly* June 1909. 309-317. Print.

# Hunter S. Thompson

## 1937-2005

Hunter Stockton Thompson is best known for authoring *Fear and Loathing in Las Vegas (1971)* and his hard-driving lifestyle, which included the steady use of drugs and firearms; making him a counterculture icon who was particularly popular among the college-age population.

Thompson was born on July 18, 1937 in Louisville, Kentucky to a middle-class family. After his father died and left the family in poverty, Thompsom had a turbulent childhood. He failed to finish high school and as a young man was incarcerated briefly for aiding and abetting a robbery. After his release, he joined the United States Air Force in 1956.

Thompson got his first exposure to journalism as a sports reporter for an Air Force newspaper at Eglin Air Force Base in Florida. After his discharge in 1958, he pursued journalism as a career and landed a series of jobs at a variety of small-town newspapers, as well as a short stint as a copy boy at *Time Magazine*.

Hunter S. Thompson wrote in his landmark article "The Kentucky Derby is Decadent and Depraved:"

> *Total chaos, no way to see the race, not even the track... nobody cares. Big lines at the outdoor betting windows, then stand back to watch winning numbers flash on the big board, like a giant bingo game. Old blacks arguing about bets; "hold on there, I'll handle this" (waving pint of whiskey, fistful of dollar bills); girl riding piggyback, T-shirt says, "Stolen from Fort Lauderdale Jail." Thousands of teenagers, group singing "Let the Sun Shine In," ten soldiers guarding the American flag, and a huge fat drunk wearing a blue football jersey (No. 80) reeling around with quart of beer in hand. No booze sold out here, too dangerous... no bathrooms either. Muscle Beach... Woodstock... many cops with riot sticks, but no sign of riot. Far across the track the clubhouse looks like a postcard from the Kentucky Derby.*

With this article, which appeared in the short-lived *Scanlan Monthly* (June, 1970), Louisville native Hunter S. Thompson was credited with creating "Gonzo journalism—" a new, highly personal style of reporting that allowed the writer to become so involved in the story that they become a central character, chronicling cultural shifts as an astute observer, and on the lookout for anything that featured American hypocrisy in the 1960s and 1970s. Biographer William McKeen noted that, because of the story's legendary status and *Scanlan's* small circulation, the story was "one of the most famous and least read articles in Thompson's career."

Thompson's rambling first-person Derby story was more about the experience of watching the crowd at the race than the actual race. At the time, the piece was hailed as a breakthrough in journalism. Thompson was inundated with fan mail and phone calls, which he said was like, "falling down an elevator shaft and landing in a pool of mermaids."

In his first book, *Hell's Angels: A Strange and Terrible Saga* (1967), Thompson, in typical "Gonzo" style, chronicled his time infiltrating the Hell's Angels motorcycle gang, "I was no longer sure whether I was doing research on the Hell's Angels or being slowly absorbed by them."

In 1970, Thompson unsuccessfully ran for sheriff of Pitkin County, Colorado, on the "Freak Power Movement" ticket. His story about the campaign experience, "The Battle of Aspen," was his first of many contributions to *Rolling Stone* magazine. He was National Affairs Editor of the Magazine until 1999.

In 1971, what began as an assignment for *Sports Illustrated* turned into *Fear and Loathing in Las Vegas: A Savage Journey to the Heart of the American Dream*, a best-selling book based on Thompson's drug-fueled journey through Las Vegas. Both a critical and commercial success, the book was adapted for film in 1998, directed by Terry Gilliam and starring Benicio del Toro and Johnny Depp (an avid big Thompson fan). Depp also starred in the 2011 film version of Thompson's, *The Rum Diary*.

*Fear and Loathing on the Campaign Trail*, a collection of Thompson's writings for *Rolling Stone* about the 1972 presidential campaign, was published in early 1973.

Thompson ended his first "Gonzo" article on the Derby by describing the chaotic scene at the end of the most famous two minutes in sports:

> *Moments after the race was over, the crowd surged wildly for the exits, rushing for cabs and busses. The next day's Courier told of violence in the parking lot; people were punched and trampled, pockets were picked, children lost, bottles hurled. But we missed all this, having retired to the press box for a bit of post-race drinking. By this time, we were both half-crazy from too much whiskey, sun fatigue, culture shock, lack of sleep and general dissolution.*

This could well have been a description of Thompson's life—he was notorious for his outrageous antics, rebellious, anti-authoritarian attitude, and unconventional reporting style. After several bouts of poor health, Thompson died of a self-inflicted gunshot wound on February 20, 2005 at his compound in Woody Creek, Colorado, near Aspen. In August 2005, a private ceremony commemorating his life was held, and Thompson's ashes were shot from a cannon topped with a clinched fist while Bob Dylan's "Mr. Tambourine Man" played in the background— all bankrolled by his friend Johnny Depp and attended by celebrities Jack Nicholson, John Cusack, Sean Penn, Bill Murray, and others.

## Sources

Editorial. *The Guardian* 22 Feb. 2005. Online. Accessed 14 April 2015.
   <http://www.theguardian.com/news/2005/feb/22/
   leadersandreply.mainsection?redirection=guardian>.

Homberger, Eric. "Hunter S Thompson." *The Guardian* 22 Feb. 2005.
   Online. Accessed 20 Dec. 2014.
   <https://www.theguardian.com/news/2005/feb/22/
   guardianobituaries.booksobituaries>.

_____. "Obituary." *The Guardian* 22 February 2005. Accessed 14
   April 2015.
   <http://www.theguardian.com/news/2005/feb/22
   /guardianobituaries.booksobituaries?redirection=guardian>.

Hoover, S. "Hunter S. Thompson and gonzo Journalism: A Research
   Guide. *Reference Review.* 37:3 (2009). 326-339. Print.

Hunter S Thompson. *Biblio.com.* Online. Accessed 22 Feb. 2014.
   <http://www.biblio.com/hunter-s-thompson/author/525>.

"Hunter S Thompson." *The Telegraph* 22 Feb. 2005. Online.
   Accessed 20 Dec. 2014.
   <http://www.telegraph.co.uk/news/obituaries/
   1484054/Hunter-S-Thompson.html>.

"Hunter S. Thompson: Biography." *bio.* Online. Accessed 20 Dec.
   2014.
   <http://www.b<iography.com/people/
   hunter-s-thompson-9506260#synopsis>.

"Hunter S. Thompson: Biography>" *IMDb.* Online. Accessed 20 Dec.
   2014.
   <http://www.imdb.com/name/nm0860219/bio>

Jackson, S. M. "The Hunter Thompson Saga. A Savage Burlesque in
   Three Parts." *Commonwealth Times*: 1, 11-14, 16, 23. 28
   Nov. 1978: Print.

Ronson, Jon. "I've Gotta Get My Elephant Tusks Back." *The
   Guardian* 22 Feb. 2005. Online. Accessed 14 April 2015.
   <http://www.theguardian.com/books/2005/feb/22/
   huntersthompson?redirection=guardian>.

Smith-Peters. "Hunter Stockton Thompson." *The Kentucky Encyclopedia*. Ed. John Kleber. Lexington, KY: U P of Kentucky, 1992. 880-881. Print.

Steadman, Ralph. "Depraved and Decadent: Adventures with Thompson." *The Guardian* 21 Feb. 2005. Online. Accessed 14 Apr. 2015. <http://www.theguardian.com/books/2005/feb/22/news.features11?redirection=guardian>.

Taylor, Kate. Truth is Weirder Than Any Fiction I've Seen..." *The Guardian* 21 Feb. 2005. Online. Accessed 14 Apr. 2015. <http://www.theguardian.com/books/2005/feb/21/huntersthompson1?redirection=guardian>.

Thompson, Hunter S. "In His Own Words: A Selection of Best-Remembered Quotes from the Master of the One-Liner." *The Guardian* 21 Feb. 2005. Online. Accessed 14 Apr. 2015. <http://www.theguardian.com/books/2005/feb/21/huntersthompson?redirection=guardian>.

Wenner, Jann S. and Corey Seymour, Eds. *Gonzo: The Life of Hunter S. Thompson, an Oral Biography* (with an introduction by Johnny Depp). New York: Little, Brown, & Co., 2007. Print.

Yates, Robert. "And Then He Missed Me." *The Guardian* 26 February 2005. Online. Accessed 14 April 2015. <http://www.theguardian.com/books/2005/feb/27/society?redirection=guardian>.

## Selected Bibliography

### Gonzo Journalism

*Hell's Angels: The Strange and Terrible Saga of the Outlaw Motorcycle Gangs*. New York: Random House, 1967. Print.

*Fear and Loathing in Las Vegas*. New York: Random House, 1971. Print.

*Fear and Loathing on the Campaign Trail '72*. San Francisco: Straight Arrow Books, 1973. Print.

*The Great Gonzo Papers, Vol. 1: The Great Shark Hunt: Strange Tales from a Strange Time*. New York: Summit Books, 1979. Print.

*The Curse of Lono* (illustrated by Ralph Steadman). New York: Bantam, 1983. Print.

*Gonzo Papers, Vol. 2: Generation of Swine: Tales of Shame and Degradation in the '80s.* New York: Summit Books, 1988. Print.

*Gonzo Papers, Vol. 3: Songs of the Doomed: More Notes on the Death of the American Dream.* New York: Simon & Schuster, 1990. Print.

*Gonzo Papers, Vol. 4: Better Than Sex: Confessions of a Political Junkie.* New York: Random House, 1994. Print.

*Mistah Leary– He Dead.* New Orleans: X-Ray Book Company, 1996. Print.

*The Fear and Loathing Letters, Vol. 1: The Proud Highway: The Saga of a Desperate Southern Gentleman 1955–1967.* New York: Random House, 1997. Print.

*The Rum Diary.* New York: Simon & Schuster, 1998. Print.

*Screw-Jack.* New York: Simon & Schuster, 2000. Print.

*Fear and Loathing in America: The Brutal Odyssey of an Outlaw Journalist 1968–1976.* New York: Simon & Schuster, 2000. Print.

*Kingdom of Fear: Loathsome Secrets of a Star-Crossed Child in the Final Days of the American Century.* New York: Simon & Schuster, 2003. Print.

*Hey Rube: Blood Sport, the Bush Doctrine, and the Downward Spiral of Dumbness: Modern History from the Sports Desk.* New York: Simon & Schuster, 2004. Print.

*Happy Birthday, Jack Nicholson.* New York: Penguin Books, 2005.

*Gonzo: Photographs by Hunter S. Thompson.* Los Angeles: AMMO Books, 2006. Print.

*The Mutineer: Rants, Ravings, and Missives from the Mountaintop 1977–2005.* New York: Simon & Schuster, 2008. Print.

*Fear and Loathing at Rolling Stone: The Essential Writings of Hunter S. Thompson.* New York: Simon & Schuster, 2011. Print.

**Selected Magazine Articles**

"The Temptations of Jean-Claude Killy." *Scanlon's Monthly* March
1970. 89-100. Print.

"The Kentucky Derby is Decadent and Depraved. *Scanlon's Monthly*
June 1970: 1-12. Print.

"Freak Power in the Rockies." *Rolling Stone* 1 October 1970: 30-
37. Print.

"Strange Rumblings in Aztlan." *Rolling Stone* 29 April 1971: 30-
37. Print.

"Memo from the Sports Desk: The So-Called 'Jesus Freak Scare'"
(as Raoul Duke). *Rolling Stone* 11 November 1971: 24.
Print.

"Fear and Loathing in Las Vegas: A Savage Journey to the Heart
of the American Dream(as Raoul Duke)." *Rolling Stone* 11
November 1971: 36-48. Print.

"Conclusion of Fear and Loathing in Las Vegas: A Savage Journey
to the Heart of the American Dream" (as Raoul Duke). *Rolling
Stone* 25 November 1971: 38-50. Print.

"The Great Shark Hunt." *Playboy*. December 1974: 183-184. Print.

"He Was a Crook: The Death of Richard Nixon." *Rolling Stone* 16
June 1994. Print.

**Short Fiction**

"Fire in the Nuts." Tucson: Gonzo International/Steam Press
Sylph Publications, 2004. Print.

# CHAPTER FOUR
## 2016

# James Lane Allen

## 1829-1925

James Lane Allen has the distinction of being called Kentucky's first important novelist. His appeal was international and he was widely read in Great Britain and the United States. He belongs to a period of the late 19th Century local color era, characterized by a focus on capturing local color and emphasizing regional dialect and vernacular. The *Oxford Companion to American Literature* says that this movement was under the dual influence of romanticism and realism. Authors in this era looked to distant places and eccentric customs, painting them with exotic scenes filled with detailed accuracy. Critics of this movement purported that it was dominated by nostalgia and sentimentality.

Allen's writing roots began with literary criticism, but after the publication of *Flute and Violin & Other Kentucky Stories* (1891), he forged a highly successful career in fiction, travel writing, and drama. He published twenty books in a career spanning 34 years. He was a contributor to many of the prominent magazines of his time, including: *Harper's Magazine, Century Magazine,* and *The Atlantic Monthly.*

Allen was born in 1829 on a farm near Lexington, Kentucky where he was exposed to a genteel life in the antebellum South. By his early 20s, the Civil War and reconstruction had altered the world in which he had been reared. This created a distinct division in the themes of his work. James Klotter, Kentucky historian, says that six of his first eight novels was of that "... idealistic, romantic world filled with stories of honor and chivalry, where gallant and noble gentlemen courted women of spotless virtue." The second half of his work was set in "... industrial America where, it seemed, ethics were replaced by greed, honor by corruption, purity by vulgarity."

Many of his novels were controversial, dealing with seldom discussed subjects for the time: Darwinism, religious doubt, sex, infidelity, and a breaking with prevailing codes of honor.

He graduated from Kentucky University (now Transylvania University) at Lexington, Kentucky in 1872 and finished a Master's degree there in 1877. He taught at various schools in Kentucky, Missouri, and West Virginia. In an effort to promote his writing career, Allen moved to New York City in 1893.

His novel, *A Kentucky Cardinal*, was released in 1894, making him a commercial as well as a critical success. A best-selling novel, *The Choir Invisible*, followed in 1897. His last published book, *The Landmark*, coincided with his death in 1925. Literary critic George Brosi says that "Although his works were very pleasing in their flowing style, they were also substantive, dealing with important themes of the day, often at the cutting edge of discourse." Other critics have suggested that he was among the last to promote the themes of pre-Civil War gentry in the South.

When *The Choir Invisible* was released in 1897, it received high praise. William Morton Payne wrote in the *Dial*: "Hardly since Hawthorne have we had such pages as the best of these." Bliss Carmen wrote in the *Boston Transcript*: "There are two chief reasons why Mr. Allen seems to be the first of our novelists today... he has a prose style of wonderful beauty, conscientiousness and simplicity... He has the inexorable conscience of the artist [;] he always gives us his best."

Allen died February 19, 1925 in New York City and is buried in the Lexington Cemetery at Lexington, Kentucky.

### Sources

Bennett, Enoch Arnold. "Mr. James Lane Allen." *Fame and Fiction.* London: Grant Richards, 1901. 171-180. Print.

Bottorff, William K. *James Lane Allen.* New York: Twayne Publishers, 1964. Print.

Brosi, George. "James Lane Allen." *KYLIT—A Site Devoted to Kentucky Writers* 25 Sept. 1997. Online. Accessed 12 Dec. 2016. <https://web.archive.org/web/19980213183808/http://www.english.eku.edu/services/kylit/allen.htm>.

"James Lane Allen." *Kentucky in American Letters Vol. II.* Ed. John Wilson Townsend. Cedar Rapids, IA: The Torch Press, 1913. 4-17. Print.

"James Lane Allen: A Sketch of His Life and Work." New York: The Macmillan Company, ?. *Kentucky Digital Library*. Online. Accessed 21 Dec. 2016. <http://kdl.kyvl.org/catalog/xt7wwp9t271q_1?>.

Klotter, James C. "Allen James Lane." *The Kentucky Encyclopedia*. Ed. John Kleber. Lexington: U P of Kentucky, 1992. 14. Print.

Knight, Grant C. *James Lane Allen and the Genteel Tradition*. Chapel Hill: U of North Carolina P, 1935. Print.

Townsend, John Wilson. *James Lane Allen: A Personal Note*. Louisville, KY: Courier-Journal Job Printing, Co., 1928. Print.

## Selected Bibliography
### Collections/Travel Writing

*The Blue-Grass Region of Kentucky & Other Articles*. New York: Harper & Brothers, 1892. Print.

*Mountain Passes of the Cumberland*. Lexington, KY: King Library Press, 1972. Print.

### Drama

*One Night in the Garden: A play in One Act*. Charlottesville: Michie, 1919. Print.

### Novels

*John Gray: A Kentucky Tale of Olden Time*. Philadelphia: Lippincott, 1893. Print.

*A Kentucky Cardinal*. New York: Harper & Brothers, 1894. Print.

*Aftermath: Second Half of a Kentucky Cardinal*. New York: Harper & Brothers, 1895. Print.

*Summer in Arcady*. New York: Macmillan Company, 1896. Print.

*The Choir Invisible*. New York: The Macmillan Company, 1897. Print.

*Two Gentlemen of Kentucky*. New York: Harper & Brothers, 1899. Print.

*The Reign of Law: A Tale of the Kentucky Hemp Fields*. New York: The Macmillan Company, 1900. Print.

*Increasing Purpose*. New York: Macmillan, 1900. Print.

*The Mettle of the Pasture*. New York: The Macmillan Company,
    1903. Print.

*The Bride of the Mistletoe*. New York: The Macmillan Company,
    1909. Print.

*The Doctor's Christmas Eve*. New York: The Macmillan Company,
    1910. Print.

*The Heroine in Bronze: A Pastoral of the City*. New York:
    Macmillan Company, 1912. Print.

*The Last Christmas Tree: An Idyl of Immortality*. Portland, ME:
    Thomas Bird Mosher, 1914. Print.

*The Sword of Youth*. New York: The Century Co., 1915. Print.

*A Cathedral Singer*. New York: The Century Co., 1916. Print.

*The Kentucky Warbler*. New York: Doubleday, Page & Co., 1918. Print.

*The Emblems of Fidelity: A Comedy of Letters*. New York:
    Doubleday, Page & Co., 1919. Print.

*The Alabaster Box*. New York: Harper & Brothers, 1923. Print.

*The Landmark*. New York: Macmillan, 1925. Print.

**Short Stories**

*Flute and Violin*. New York: Harper & Brothers, 1891. Print.

*Nuggets from James Lane Allen* (*Christmas Classics Series*). New
    York: Base & Hopkins, 1920. Print.

*The Landmark*. New York: The Macmillan Company, 1925.

# Harlan Hubbard

## 1900-1988

Harlan Hubbard's realization that industrialism and consumerism posed a threat to the environment and to human survival, changed his life forever. So did his marriage to Anna Eikenhout in 1943, his subsequent 1944 launch of a shanty boat onto the Ohio River in Northern Kentucky for an eight year-long adventure, and his return to live a Thoreauvian life at Payne Hollow in Trimble County, Kentucky.

When writer and director Morgan Atkinson produced the 2012 documentary, "Wonder: The Lives of Harlan and Anna Hubbard," she declared: "What Henry David Thoreau did for two years Anna and Harlan Hubbard did for forty except they did it in the 20th century. Anna and Harlan chose to live life as few people in modern times have. In so doing they inspired thousands."

Anna and Harlan welcomed countless numbers of visitors to their humble abode on the river. Sometimes, entire classes of college students studying botany, writing, art, music, or utopian societies came to visit. Some just came to help in the everyday chores of gardening, cutting firewood, cooking, or helping check Harlan's trot-lines on the river.

Harlan was born in 1900 at Bellvue, a city in Northern Kentucky opposite Cincinnati, Ohio. After the death of his father in 1907, he moved to New York City when he was eight years old to be with two older brothers. He was educated at Childs High School in the Bronx, the New York National Academy of Design, and the Art Academy of Cincinnati.

Although Harlan and Anna were well known for their Thoreauvian lifestyle, Harlan is best known as a writer. His books *Shantyboat* and *Shantyboat in the Bayous* document their river journeys; while *Payne Hollow* and *Journals, 1929-1944* related his philosophy of the well-lived life.

Harlan published twelve books from 1953-1996, including: journals, travel essays, and artwork (woodcuts and paintings) with publishers such as Dodd-Mead, Eakins Press, Oyo Press, Larkspur Press, Gnomon Press, and The University Press of Kentucky.

Officials at the Kentucky Museum of Art and Craft have said of Harlan Hubbard:

> In the tradition of naturalists like Thoreau, Muir
> and Abbey, Kentuckian Harlan Hubbard began to
> live a life of communing with nature, not fearing it.
> Harlan and his wife Anna became new prophets

*of environmentalism and sustainability, and made
it their concerted mission to fully explore the sym-
biotic relationship of humans to the natural world.*

Anna passed in 1986 and Harlan in 1988. They
bequeathed Payne Hollow to Paul Hassfurder, an artist they
befriended.

## Sources

Berry, Wendell. *Harlan Hubbard: Life and Work*. Lexington, KY:
    U P of Kentucky, 1990. Print.

Caddell, Bill. "Harlan Hubbard Artwork." Online. Accessed 22
    Dec. 2016.
    <http://www.dcwi.com/hubbard/bio.html>.

"Harlan Hubbard: A Life on the Fringe of Society." *Harlan
    Hubbard.com*. Online. Accessed 22 Dec. 2016.
    <http://harlanhubbard.com/>.

"Harlan Hubbard." *The Kentucky Encyclopedia*. Ed. John E.
    Kleber. Lexington, KY: U P of Kentucky, 1992. 444. Print.

Mayhew, Chris. "NKY preserving artist Harlan Hubbard's Legacy."
    *Community Press.com*. 14 March 2016. Online. Accessed 22
    Dec. 2016. <http://www.cincinnati.com/story/news/local/ft-
    thomas/2016/03/07/nky-preserving-artist-harlan-hubbards-
    legacy/81459332/>.

Wallis, Don. *Harlan Hubbard and the River: A Visionary Life*.
    Yellow Springs, OH: OYO Press, 1989. Print.

## Selected Bibliography

**Artwork/Illustrations**

*The Woodcuts of Harlan Hubbard: From the Collection of Bill
    Caddell*. Lexington, KY: U P of Kentucky, 1994. Print.

**Autobiographical/Essays**

*Payne Hollow: Life on the Fringe of Society*. New York: Eakins
    Press, 1974. Print.

*Payne Hollow: Life on the Fringe of Society*. Frankfort, KY:
    Gnomon Press, 1997. Print.

**Biographical**

*A Visit with Harlan Hubbard* (with Wade H. Hall). Lexington, KY:
    University of Kentucky Libraries, 1996. Print.

**Collections**

"Payne Hollow" in *Kentucky Renaissance: An Anthology of
    Contemporary Writing*. Ed. Jonathan Greene. Lexington, KY:
    Gnomon Press, 1976. Print.

*Oyo: An Ohio River Anthology Vol. I* (with Don Wallis). Yellow
    Springs, OH: Oyo Press, 1987. Print.

**Drama**

*Sonata at Payne Hollow: A Play* (with Wendell Berry). Monterey,
    KY: Larkspur Press, 2001. Print.

**Travel/Journals/Autobiographical**

*Shantyboat*. New York: Dodd, Mead, 1953. Print.

*Shantyboat: A River Way of Life*. Lexington, KY: U P of Kentucky,
    1977. Print.

*Harlan Hubbard Journals, 1929-1944*. Lexington, KY: U P of
    Kentucky, 1987. Print.

*Shantyboat on the Bayous*. Lexington, KY: U P of Kentucky, 1990.
    Print.

*Shantyboat Journal*. Lexington, KY: U P of Kentucky, 1994. Print.

*Payne Hollow Journal*. Lexington, KY: U P of Kentucky, 1996. Print.

Photograph by James B. Goode.

# Bobbie Ann Mason

## 1940-

Western Kentucky native Bobbie Ann Mason has been writing and publishing since the 1970s. Her first book publication was her dissertation *Nabokov's Garden: A Guide to Ada* (1974). To date, she has published seventeen volumes including five novels, seven collections of short fiction, one memoir, one biography, and two works of literary criticism. Her publishers include: Harper and Row, HarperCollins, Random House, and others.

Mason said of her of her fiction: "I grew so sick of reading about the alienated hero of superior sensibility who so frequently dominates 20th Century American literature that I decided to write fiction about the antithesis." As a result, she is known for launching a movement in fiction known as "Shopping Mall Realism," because of its focus on everyday characters and realistic regional dialogue.

Mason is frequently labeled as a minimalist or "dirty" realist, and most identifies with what John Barth called "... blue-collar hyper-realist super minimalist." Mason has said that her style "comes out of a way of hearing people talk." Many of her stories place characters at transitional points in their lives where they are forced to make hard decisions. David Quammen of the *New York Times Book Review* said:

> *Loss and deprivation, the disappointment of pathet-ically modest hopes, are the themes Bobbie Ann Mason works and reworks. She portrays the disquieted lives of men and women not blessed with much money or education or luck, but cursed with enough sensitivity and imagination to suffer regrets.*

Her most critically acclaimed book is the short story collection *Shiloh and Other Stories* (1982). Novelist Ann Tyler hailed her in the *New Republic* as "... a full-fledged master of the short story." Robert Towers in *The New York Review of Books* said, "Bobbie Ann Mason is one of those rare writers who, by concentrating their attention on a few square miles of native turf, are able to open up new and surprisingly wide worlds for the delighted reader." Another critic characterized this work as describing, "... the lives of working-class people in a shifting rural society dominated by chain stores, television, and superhighways." Her stories have appeared in: *New Yorker, Atlantic Monthly, Paris Review, Harper's, Southern Review, Mother Jones,* and other nationally recognized magazines.

Mason's awards include: *Best American Short Stories* (1981), Ernest Hemingway Foundation Award for Outstanding First Works of Fiction (*Shiloh and Other Stories*, 1983), *Best American Short Stories* (1983), The Penn/Hemingway Award (*Shiloh and Other Stories*, 1983), National Book Critics Circle Award for Fiction Finalist (*Shiloh and Other Stories*, 1983), National Book Award Finalist (*Shiloh and Other Stories*, 1983), PEN/Faulkner Award Finalist (Shiloh and Other Stories, 1983), The National Endowment for the Arts Award (1983), Guggenheim Fellowship (1984), Pushcart Prize (1984), two time winner of the O Henry Award (1986 & 1988), National Book Critics Circle Award finalist for Fiction (*Feather Crowns*, 1993), Pushcart Prize (1996), Pulitzer Prize finalist in Biography (*Clear Springs*, 1999), and The Southern Book Award for Fiction (*Zigzagging Down a Wild Trail*, 2002).

Mason graduated from the University of Kentucky (B.A., 1962), the State University of New York at Binghamton (M.A., 1966) and the University of Connecticut, Storrs (Ph.D., 1972).

### Sources

"About Bobbie Ann Mason." *Bobbie Ann Mason*. Online. Accessed 1 Jan. 2017. <http://www.bobbieannmason.net/bio.htm>.

Aycock-Simpson, Judy. "Bobbie Ann Mason's Portrayal of Modern Western Kentucky." *Border States: Journal of the Kentucky-Tennessee American Studies Association*. 7 (1989). Online. Accessed 1 Jan. 2017. <http://spider.georgetowncollege.edu/htallant/border/bs7/aycock-s.htm>.

"Bobbie Ann Mason: Highlights from the Archives." *New York Times*. Online. Accessed 1 Jan. 2017. <http://topics.nytimes.com/top/reference/timestopics/people/m/bobbie_ann_mason/index.html>.

"Featured Author: Bobbie Ann Mason." *Books: The New York Times*. Online. Accessed 1 Jan. 2017. <http://www.nytimes.com/books/98/08/09/specials/mason.html>.

Gholson, Craig. "Bobbie Ann Mason." *Bomb: Artists in Conversation*. 28 (Summer 1989). Online. Accessed 1 Jan. 2017. <http://bombmagazine.org/article/1218/bobbie-ann-mason>.

Hall, Wade. "Bobbie Ann Mason." *The Kentucky Encyclopedia*. Ed. John E. Kleber. Lexington, KY: The U P of Kentucky, 1992. 614. Print.

Mason, Bobbie Ann. "Interview with Bobbie Ann Mason." *The Missouri Review*. 20.3 (Fall 1997). Online. Accessed 1 Jan. 2017. <http://www.missourireview.com/archives/bbarticle/interview-with-bobby-ann-mason/>.

Pokrass, Meg. "Bobbie Ann Mason." *New World Writing*. Online. Accessed 1 Jan. 2017. <http://newworldwriting.net/back/fall-2012-2/bobbie-ann-mason/>.

## Selected Bibliography

**Biography**

*Elvis Presley*. Waterville, ME: Thorndike, 2003. Print.

**Literary Criticism**

*Nabokov's Garden: A Guide to Ada*. Ann Arbor, MI: Ardis, 1974. Print.

*The Girl Sleuth: A Feminist Guide*. Athens, GA: The U of Georgia P, 1975. Print.

**Memoir**

*Clear Springs: A Family Story*. New York: Random House, 1999. Print.

**Novels**

*In Country*. New York: Harper & Row, 1985. Print.

*Feather Crowns*. New York: HarperCollins, 1994. Print.

*Spence & Lila*. New York: HarperCollins, 1998. Print.

*An Atomic Romance*. New York: Random House, 2005. Print.

*In Country* (Reprinted). New York: Harper Perennial, 2005. Print.

*The Girl in the Blue Beret.* New York: Random House, 2011. Print.

**Short Fiction**

*Shiloh and Other Stories.* New York: HarperCollins, 1983. Print.

*Love Life.* New York: HarperCollins, 1989. Print.

*With Jazz.* Monterey, KY: Larkspur Press, 1994. Print.

*Still Life With Watermelon.* Monterey, KY: Larkspur Press, 1997. Print.

*Midnight Magic: Selected Stories.* New York: HarperCollins, 1998. Print.

*Zigzagging Down a Wild Trail: Stories.* New York: Random House, 2002. Print.

*Nancy Culpepper.* New York: Random House, 2006. Print.

# Alice Hegan Rice

## 1870-1942

Alice Hegan Rice was born in Shelbyville, Kentucky at the home of her grandfather, Judge James Caldwell. Her parents, Samuel and Sallie Caldwell Hegan lived near the Cabbage Patch Settlement in Louisville. Because of health issues, Alice was delayed starting her formal education. At the age of ten, she entered Miss Hampton's College, a private school in Louisville, where she studied writing and drawing, and general studies subjects. After graduation, she embarked on several benevolent, socio-economic, altruistic ventures with the under-privileged in the Louisville, Kentucky area.

Rice was made famous by her best-selling novel *Mrs.*

*Wiggs of the Cabbage Patch* (1901), which sold 650,000 copies in its first two years. The novel was inspired by her involvement with the city's poor children in the slum known as the "Cabbage Patch Settlement" where, at the age of 16, she served as an aide at a Presbyterian Mission Sunday school. Alice and Mary Louise Marshall, daughter of Superintendent Mission Burwell K. Marshall, founded the Cabbage Patch Settlement House in Louisville in 1910.

This novel has been reprinted over fifty times, translated into several languages, and was the basis for numerous stage, screen, and radio productions. There are four Hollywood film versions. The best known is the 1934 film starring Zausa Pitts and W. C. Fields. The last film adaptation was in 1942 and starred Oscar winning actress Fay Bainter as protagonist Mrs. Elvira Wiggs. Rice published two sequels to *Mrs. Wiggs*: *Lovely Mary* (1903) and *Mr. Opp* (1909).

Critic and Scholar Mary Boewe in her book *Beyond the Cabbage Patch: The Literary World of Alice Hegan Rice* (2010), said that in Rice's idyllic view, the reader can see in the *Wiggs* story:

> ... the obvious elements of Victorianism: the virtues of domesticity, an exaltation of motherhood, the work ethic, the evils of drink, female interdependence, child-rearing techniques, child labor concerns, social welfare programs, and the intricacies of etiquette.

Shortly after the publication of her first novel, Alice married established dramatist and poet Cale Young Rice (December 18, 1902). In 1910, they built a house in the art community of St. James Court in Louisville. The union of these writers led them to produce dozens of literary works during the next forty years.

This couple was well known in the 20th Century publishing world, which often put them at social and literary events with such iconic personalities as Mark Twain, Edith Wharton, Henry Watterson, Theodore Roosevelt, and Thornton Wilder.

In a review of Boewe's book, literary critic Wes Berry said: *Beyond the Cabbage Patch is like reading the society pages of American culture during the early decades of the twentieth century... Boewe captures the flavors of the decades—especially in Louisville—with reviews of social balls and theater events, excerpts from Alice's correspondence with editors and friends, and news of the world beyond Louisville, as when the big war begins in Europe.*

Alice published more than twenty books between 1901 and 1942, with prestigious publishers such as: The Century Company, D. Appleton-Century-Crofts, Grosset and Dunlap, and others. *Mrs. Wiggs of the Cabbage Patch* produced royalties that financed international travel to Japan, England, China, India, Korea, and Egypt, as well as vacations to California, Florida, and New York.

Critics place Alice in the Modernist era, during which she published a sub-genre of tragicomic stories about Louisville's disenfranchised tenement-dwelling poor and some sentimental fiction that was heavily influenced by her international and domestic travels and active social and family life. She also published two children's books.

Rice died February 10, 1942 and is buried in the Cave

Hill Cemetery at Louisville, Kentucky. Her autobiography *The Inky Way* was published posthumously in 1940.

## Sources

"Alice Hegan Rice." *Kentucky in American Letters Vol. II.* Ed. John Wilson Townsend. Cedar Rapids, IA: The Torch Press, 1913. 238-239. Print.

"Alice Hegan Rice." *Literature Network.* Online. Accessed 11 Jan. 2017. <http://www.online-literature.com/alice-rice/>.

Berry, Wes. "Book Review: Beyond the Cabbage Patch: The Literary World of Alice Hegan Rice." *Indiana Magazine of History.* 108:3 (2012). Online. Accessed 11 Jan. 2017. <https://scholarworks.iu.edu/journals/index.php/imh/article/view/12721/19078>.

Bowe, Mary. *Beyond the Cabbage Patch: The Literary World of Alice Hegan Rice.* Louisville, KY: Butler Books, 2010. Print.

Henson, Gail. "Alice Hegan Rice." *The Kentucky Encyclopedia.* Ed. John Kleber. Lexington, KY: U P of Kentucky. 770-771. Print.

Richey, Carolyn Leutzinger. "Book Review: Beyond the Cabbage Patch: The Literary World of Alice Hegan Rice." *Mark Twain Project.* Online. Accessed 11 Jan. 2017. <http://www.twainweb.net/reviews/Rice.html>.

## Selected Bibliography

**Autobiographical**

*The Inky Way.* New York: D. Appleton-Century Company, 1940. Print.

**Children's Books**

*Lovey Mary.* New York: The Century Company, 1903. Print.

*Captain June.* New York: The Century Company, 1907. Print.

**Devotionals**

*My Pillow Book.* New York: D. Appleton-Century Company, 1937. Print.

**Novels**

*Mrs. Wiggs of the Cabbage Patch*. New York: Grosset & Dunlap, 1901. Print.

*Sandy*. New York: The Century Company, 1905. Print.

*Mr. Opp*. New York: The Century Company, 1909. Print.

*A Romance of Billy-Goat Hill*. New York: The Century Company, 1912. Print.

*The Honorable Percival*. New York: The Century Company, 1914. Print.

*Calvary Alley*. New York: The Century Company, 1917. Print.

*Quin*. New York: The Century Company, 1921. Print.

*Winners and Losers* (with Cale Young Rice). New York: The Century Company, 1925. Print.

*The Buffer*. New York: The Century Company, 1929. Print.

*Mr. Pete & Co.* New York: D. Appleton-Century Company, 1933. Print.

*The Lark Legacy*. New York: D. Appleton-Century Company, 1935. Print.

*Our Ernie*. New York: D. Appleton-Century Company, 1939. Print.

*Happiness Road* (posthumous). New York: D. Appleton-Century Company, 1942. Print.

**Short Fiction**

*Miss Mink's Soldier and Other Stories*. New York: The Century Company, 1918. Print.

*Turn About Tales* (with Cale Young Rice). New York: The Century Company, 1920. Print.

*Passionate Follies* (with Cale Young Rice). London: Hodder & Stoughton, 1936. Print.

# Jean Ritchie

## 1922-2015

Jean Ritchie said in her book *The Singing Family of the Cumberlands*:

> *I was born in Viper, Kentucky, in the Cumberland Mountains, on the eighth day of December 1922. I think I was a little of a surprise to my mother who had thought that if a woman had a baby in her fortieth year it would be her last. Mom had my brother Wilmer when she was forty, and she settled back to raise her thirteenth young uns without any more interference. Then when she was forty-four, I came along.*

Jean was the youngest of fourteen children, who grew up in Kentucky's Cumberland Mountains where her family had lived since the 1700s. She helped raise and prepare meals by hand, learning at an early age to plant, harvest, and prepare meals. She was familiar with the use of handmade tools. Music accompanied almost every part of her family's life. Dulcimer, guitar, and fiddle music was prominent in their work, church services, weddings, and funerals.

Much of this music had roots in the British Isles and was handed down from generation to generation. As with any music and lyrics, many variations evolved. For example, there are dozens of versions of the traditional English ballad "Barbara Allen."

Ritchie said:

*It was always a wonder to me how families living close to one another could sing the same song and sing it so different. Or how one family would sing a song among themselves for years, and their neighbor family never knew that song at all. Most curious of all was how one member of a family living in a certain community could have almost a completely different set of songs than his cousins living a few miles away.*

She was a fierce promoter of these songs and frequently sang traditional ballads such as: "Barbara Allen," "The Cuckoo is a Pretty Bird," and "The Cool of the Day" in her unique, haunting, acapella soprano voice. Audiences often reported that the hair stood up on their necks when they heard her perform.

Jean was destined to become an iconic figure in

American folk music. She was discovered and recorded by Alan Lomax, performed at Carnegie Hall, at London's Royal Albert Hall, and at the first Newport Folk Festival (1959) in Rhode Island, along with Pete Seeger, Odetta, Sonny Terry and Brownie McGhee. She became a fixture at Greenwich Village coffeehouses, and was often on the New York radio broadcasts with folk singer Oscar Brand. She had a powerful influence on Bob Dylan and often performed with such luminaries as Doc Watson and Leadbelly. Her songs were recorded by Johnny Cash, Emmy Lou Harris, Linda Ronstadt, Judy Collins, Dolly Parton, and others.

"There is no one else in her category," Lomax told the *Louisville Courier-Journal* in 1989. "She has devoted herself to her heritage and the struggle to convey it in all its majesty and beauty."

Ritchie wrote and recorded many famous original songs, including: "Black Waters," "Blue Diamond Mines" and "The L&N Don't Stop Here Anymore." Her discography includes 33 albums recorded between 1952 and 2002.

Ritchie was a Phi Beta Kappa graduate of the University of Kentucky (1946) with a degree in Social Work. She worked, for a short while in New York at the Henry Street Settlement, an educational and social services center on the Lower East Side.

She published ten books between 1964 and 1988. Dozens of articles appeared in *Sing Out*, *Mountain Life and Work*, *The Ladies Home Journal*, and others. Countless numbers of articles were written about her, many appearing in prestigious newspapers, magazines, and books.

Ritchie married photographer and woodcraftsman George Pickow in 1950, and together they published books and music, owned a recording label, and operated a dulcimer-making shop in Port Washington, N.Y. She passed June 1, 2015 in Berea, Kentucky where she had lived since her husband's death in 2010.

## Sources

Carter-Schwendler, Karen L. and David Carter. "Mountain Born: The Jean Ritchie Story." *Kentucky Educational Television.* Online. Accessed 6 Dec. 2015. <https://www.ket.org/mountainborn/biblio.htm>.

"Jean Ruth Ritchie." *The Kentucky Encyclopedia.* Ed. John Kleber. Lexington, KY: U P of Kentucky, 1992. 773-774. Print.

Ritchie, Jean. *Singing Family of the Cumberlands.* New York: Oak Publications, 1963. Print.

Schofield, Derek. "Jean Ritchie Obituary." *The Guardian.* 3 Jun. 2015. Online. Accessed 6 Dec. 2015. <https://www.theguardian.com/music/2015/jun/03/jean-ritchie>.

Schudell, Matt. "Jean Ritchie, singer who helped lead folk revival of '50s and '60s, dies at 92." *Washington Post.* 2 Jun. 2015. Online. Accessed 6 Dec. 2015. <http://www.washingtonpost.com/entertainment/music/jean ritchie singer-who-helped-lead-folk-revival-of-50s-and-60s-dies-at-92/2015/06/02/9d2e3fc4-095e-11e5-95fd-d580f1c5d4 4e_story.html>.

Winick, Stephen. "Jean Ritchie, 1922-2015." *Folklife Today.* 11 Jun. 2015. Online. Accessed 6 Dec. 2015. <http://blogs.loc.gov/folklife/2015/06/jean-ritchie-1922-2015/>.

## Selected Bibliography
### Books: Music: Lyrics, History, Autobiography

*Apple Seeds and Soda Straws: Love Charms and Legends Written Down for Young and Old.* New York: H.Z. Walck, 1965. Print.

*Celebration of Life.* Port Washington, NY: Geordie Music
     Publishing, 1971. Print.

*The Dulcimer Book.* New York: Oak Publications, 1963. Print.

*Dulcimer People.* New York: Oak Publications, 1975. Print.

*Folk Songs of the Southern Appalachians as Sung by Jean Ritchie.*
     New York: Oak Publications, 1965. Print.

*From Fair to Fair.* New York: H.Z. Walk, 1966. Print.

*Garland of Mountain Songs.* New York: Broadcast Music, 1953.
     Print.

*Singing Family of the Cumberlands.* New York: Oxford University
     Press, 1955. Print.

_____ (reprint). New York: Oak Publications, 1963. Print.

_____ (reprint). Port Washington, NY: Geordie Music Publishing,
     1980. Print.

_____ (reprint).  Lexington: U P of Kentucky, 1988. Print.

*The Swapping Song Book.* New York: Oak Publications, 1965. Print.

*Traditional Mountain Dulcimer.* New York: Homespun Tapes, 1984.
     Print.

**Magazine Articles:**

"A Dulcimer Round from Jean Ritchie." *Sing Out!* 25/2 (1976):
     20-21. Print.

"Jean Ritchie's Junaluska Keynote: Now Is the Cool of the Day."
     *Mountain Life and Work* 46/5 (1970): 3-8. Print.

"Living Is Collecting: Growing Up in a Southern Appalachian
     'Folk' Family." *An Appalachian Symposium: Essays Written in
     Honor of Cratis D. Williams.* Ed. J.W. Williamson. 188-98.
     Boone, NC: Appalachian State UP, 1977. Print.

"Yonder Comes My Beau." *Ladies Home Journal* 72 (April 1955): 54,
     127-29. Print.

**Other Articles and Books of Interest**

Baker, Edna Ritchie. "Memories of Musical Moments." *Appalachian
     Heritage* 5:3 (1977): 59-64. Print.

"Folksongs for Singing: 'Pretty Little Pink.'" *Mountain Life and
     Work* 26:3 (1950): 13-14. Print.

"The Singing Ritchies." *Mountain Life and Work* 29:3 (1953): 6-10. Print.

Bluestein, Gene. *Poplore: Folk and Pop in American Culture.* Amherst: University of Massachusetts Press, 1994. Print.

Botkin, B.A. *The American Play-Party Song.* New York: Frederick Ungar Publishing Co., 1963. Print.

Brand, Oscar. *The Ballad Mongers: Rise of the Modern Folksong.* New York: Funk and Wagnalls, 1962. Print.

Brewer, Mary T. "A Golden Memory." *Mountain Life and Work* 40:2 (1964): 21-25. Print.

Carter-Schwendler, Karen L. *Traditional Background, Contemporary Context: The Music and Activities of Jean Ritchie to 1977.* Ph.D. Dissertation, University of Kentucky, 1995. Print.

Jones, Loyal. "Jean Ritchie: Twenty-Five Years After." *Appalachian Journal* VIII (1981): 224-229. Print.

*The Newport Folk Festival Songbook* (Introduction by Jean Ritchie). New York: Alfred Music Company, 1965. Print.

Smith, L. Allen. *A Catalogue of Pre-Revival Appalachian Dulcimers, with a Foreword by Jean Ritchie.* Columbia: U of Missouri P, 1983. Print.

*Transforming Tradition: Folk Music Revivals Examined.* Ed. Neil V. Rosenberg. Urbana and Chicago: U of Illinois P, 1993. Print.

# CHAPTER FIVE
## 2017

# Irvin Shrewsbury Cobb

## 1876-1944

Paducah native Irvin Shrewsbury Cobb was perhaps one of Kentucky's most versatile writers and personalities from the 1920s to 1940s. Journalist, essayist, syndicated columnist, novelist, poet, script writer, actor, storyteller, humorist, lecturer, and Academy Awards host were among the many roles Cobb played in a career that spanned over 50 years.

As a journalist, he wrote for the *Paducah Daily News*, *Louisville Evening Post*, *The New York Evening Sun*, *The New York Evening World*, *Cincinnati Post*, and *Saturday Evening Post*.

Cobb was ardently anti-prohibition and a prominent member of the Association Against the Prohibition Amendment

(AAPA) founded in 1919 by Capt. W.H. Slayton, a retired naval officer. The Association and its two most prominent members were credited as primaries in the demise of Prohibition in 1934. His crusade prompted one of his most famous novels *Red Likker* (1929) which was touted as being the only American novel ever devoted completely to the whiskey industry. The novel is set in post-Civil War and focuses upon an old Kentucky family headed by Colonel Atilla Bird who operates Bird & Son distillery until the advent of Prohibition in 1920. Cobb once lamented that prior to Prohibition, "Men of all stations of life drank freely and with no sense of shame in their drinking... Bar-rail instep, which is a fallen arch reversed, was a common complaint among us."

Cobb was the author of sixty-nine published books, including novels, short stories, essays, memoirs, and collections of newspaper and magazine articles. His first book *Talks with the Fat Chauffer* debuted in 1909 and his last, *Piano Jim and the Impotent Pumpkin Vine*, was released posthumously in 1950. Although many of his works have a serious bent, most were comedic, and infused with a healthy dose of rural Kentucky wit and hyperbolic humor.

In addition to his fame as a war correspondent, newspaper editor, and radio personality, Cobb became involved in the movie industry when three of his short stories were adapted to the screen in 1921. "All American Storytellers (an experimental sound short)," "Peck's Bad Boy," and "Pardon my French" were all released that year. He continued writing for the film industry well into the 1930s.

"The Woman Accused," starring Cary Grant and Nancy Carroll was released in 1933. He received more critical acclaim when he was paired with director John Ford, who made two major films based on his work. The first film, "Judge Priest" (1934), starred Will Rogers in the title role, with Cobb himself in a small part, and was filmed by Fox Studios.

The second, "The Sun Shines Bright," was released by Republic Studios in 1953, nine years after Cobb's death. This was the most elaborate of Ford's Cobb films and was based on three specific stories: "The Sun Shines Bright," "The Mob from Massac," and "The Lord Provides." The film cast Charles Winninger as Judge Billy Priest. One other film appeared in the interim, director John Ford's "Steamboat Round The Bend" starved Will Rogers and Anne Shirley with Cobb cast as Captain Eli.

During Cobb's acting career, he appeared in ten movies between 1932 and 1938. His major roles were in "Pepper, Everybody' Old Man" (1936) and "Hawaii Calls" (1938). He was selected to host the 6th Academy Awards in 1935.

Critic H.L. Mencken compared Cobb to Mark Twain. He also garnered respect from such well-known writers as Joel Chandler Harris, but Cobb's literary reputation faded rapidly at the turn of the 1940s. Many critics have suggested that Cobb's writing was caught in the wake of post-Civil War, when "His benign vision of the rural south no longer seemed relevant or accessible amid the rising of the civil rights movement and the call for an end to segregation." Cobbs style, like many of the local color era writers grew increasingly dated and out-of-step with contemporary writing.

After a period of declining health, Cobb died March 10, 1944 and is buried in Oak Grove Cemetery at Paducah, Kentucky.

## Sources

Eder, Bruce. "Irvin S. Cobb Biography." *Fandango*. Online.
Accessed 25 Nov. 2016.
<http://www.fandango.com/people/irvin-s-cobb-127838/biography>.

"Irvin S. Cobb." *FantasticFiction*. Online. Accessed 25 Nov.
2016.
<https://www.fantasticfiction.com/c/irvin-s-cobb/>.

"Irvin S. Cobb." *Kentucky in American Letters Vol. II*. Ed.
John Wilson Townsend. Cedar Rapids, IA: The Torch Press,
1913. 323-327. Print.

"Irvin S. Cobb." *Wikipedia*. Online. Accessed 25 Nov. 2016.
<https://en.wikipedia.org/wiki/Irvin_S._Cobb>.

Lawson, Anita. *Irvin S. Cobb*. Bowling Green, OH: Bowling Green
State University Popular Press, Ohio, 1984. Print.

Lawson, Anita. "Irvin Shrewsbury Cobb." *The Kentucky
Encyclopedia*. Ed. John Kleber. Lexington, Ky.: U P of
Kentucky, 1992. 211-212. Print.

Sullivan, Jack. "Who in the Heck is Was Irvin S. Cobb?" *Bottles
and Extras* Summer 2006: 38. Online. Accessed 23 Nov. 2016.
<http://www.fohbc.org/PDF_Files/IrvinSCobb_JSullivan.pdf>.

## Selected Bibliography

### Autobiography/Memoir

*The Red Glutton: With the German Army at the Front*. London:
Hodder & Stoughton, 1915. Print.

*Paths of Glory*. New York: George H. Doran Company, 1915. Print.

*Speaking of Prussians*. New York: George H. Doran Company, 1917.
Print.

*Stickfuls: Compositions of a Newspaper Minion*. New York: George
H. Doran Company, 1923. Print.

*Exit Laughing*. Indianapolis: Bobbs-Merrill, 1941. Print.

### Collections

*The Works of Irvin S. Cobb*. New York: Review of Reviews, 1923. Print.

*Irvin Cobb at His Best*. New York: Doubleday Doran, 1929. Print.

*Cobb's Cavalcade: A Selection from the Writings of Irvin S. Cobb*. Cleveland, OH: The World Publishing Company, 1945. Print.

## Essays

*Paths of Glory*. New York: George H. Doran Company, 1915. Print.

*What the Victory or Defeat of Germany Means to Every American*. New York: National Security League, 1917. Print.

*Oh, Well, You Know How Women Are* (with Mary Robert)! New York: George H. Doran Company, 1920. Print.

*From Place to Place: Stories About Themselves*. New York: George H. Doran Company, 1920. Print.

*A Plea For Old Cap Collier*. New York: George H. Doran Company, 1921. Print.

*Both Sides of the Street*. New York: Cosmopolitan Corporation, 1930. Print.

*One Way to Stop a Panic*. New York: Robert M. McBride & Company, 1933. Print.

## History

*The Lost Irish Tribes in the South*. Washington, D.C.: Irish National Bureau, 1919. Print.

## Humor

*Cobb's Anatomy*. New York: George H. Doran Company, 1912. Print.

*Roughing It DeLuxe*. New York: Cosmopolitan, 1914. Print.

*Europe Revised*. New York: George H. Doran Company, 1914. Print.

*Eating in Two or Three Languages*. New York: George H. Doran Company, 1919. Print.

*A Plea for Old Cap Collier*. New York: George H. Doran Company, 1921. Print.

*Indiana: Intellectually She Rolls Her Own*. New York: George H. Doran Company, 1924. Print.

*Kansas: Shall We Civilize Her or Let Her Civilize Us?* New York: George H. Doran Company, 1924. Print.

*Kentucky The Proud State*. New York: George H. Doran Company, 1924. Print.

*Maine: A State of Ruggedness*. New York: George H. Doran Company, 1924. Print.

*New York*. New York: George H. Doran Company, 1924. Print.

*North Carolina: All She Needs is a Press Agent*. New York: George H. Doran, 1924. Print.

*Here Comes the Bride*. New York: George H. Doran Company, 1925. Print.

*Many Laughs for Many Days*. New York: George H. Doran Company, 1925. Print.

Cobb, Irvin, et al. *Around the World With Rudyard Kipling*. New York: Doubleday, Page and Company, 1926. Print.

*All Aboard: Saga of a Romantic River*. New York: Cosmopolitan Corp., 1929. Print.

*To Be Taken Before Sailing*. New York: Cosmopolitan Book Company, 1930. Print.

*Down Yonder With Judge Priest and Irvin Cobb*. New York: Ray Long & Richard Smith, 1932. Print.

*Four Useful Pups*. Chicago: Rand McNally, 1940. Print.

*Glory, Glory, Hallelujah!*. Indianapolis: Bobbs-Merrill, 1941. Print.

**Miscellaneous Non-Fiction**

*The Glory of the Coming*. New York: George H. Doran, 1918. Print.

*The Abandoned Farmers* (Humorous non-fiction). New York: George H. Doran, 1920. Print.

*Incredible Truth* (News Articles, Diaries, Documents, etc.). New York: Cosmopolitan Book Company, 1931. Print.

*Irvin S. Cobb's Own Recipe Book* (Cocktail Recipes). Louisville, KY: Frankfort Distilleries, Inc., 1934. Print.

**Novels**

*Back Home: Being the Narrative of Judge Priest and His People*. New York: George H. Doran Company, 1912. Print.

*Cobb's Bill of Fare*. New York: George H. Doran Company, 1912. Print.

*Speaking of Operations*. New York: Doubleday, Doran & Company, 1915. Print.

*Old Judge Priest*. New York: George H. Doran Company, 1916. Print.

*Fibble D. D.* New York: George H. Doran Company, 1916. Print.

*Those Times and These*. New York: George H. Doran Company, 1917. Print.

*The Thunders of Silence*. New York: George H. Doran Company, 1918. Print.

*The Life of the Party*. New York: George H. Doran Company, 1919. Print.

*J. Poindexter, Colored*. New York: George H. Doran Company, 1922. Print.

*A Laugh a Day Keeps the Doctor Away*. New York: George H. Doran Company, 1923. Print.

*Alias Ben Alibi*. New York: George H. Doran Company, 1925. Print.

*Some United States*. New York: George H. Doran Company, 1926. Print.

*Chivalry Peak*. New York: Cosmopolitan Book Corporation, 1927. Print.

*Red Likker: A Novel of Old and New Kentucky*. New York: Cosmopolitan Book Corporation, 1929. Print.

*This Man's World*. New York: Cosmopolitan Book Corporation, 1929. Print.

*Murder Day by Day*. London: Cassell, 1934. Print.

*There is Such a Place*. ? 1934. Print.

*Judge Priest Turns Detective*. Indianapolis: Bobbs-Merrill Company, 1937. Print.

**Short Stories**

*Back Home*. New York: Grossett & Dunlap, 1912. Print.

*The Escape of Mr. Trimm: His Plight and Other Plights*. New York: George H. Doran Company, 1913. Print.

*Speaking of Operations*. New York: George H. Doran Company, 1915. Print.

*From Place to Place*. New York: George H. Doran Company, 1920. Print.

*The Snake Doctor*. New York: George H. Doran Company, 1923. Print.

*Goin' on Fourteen*. New York: George H. Doran Company, 1924. Print.

*My Stories That I Like Best* (with James Oliver, et al). New York:
Cosmopolitan Book Corporation, 1925. Print.

*Prose and Cons*. New York: George H. Doran, 1926. Print.

*On an Island That Cost $24.00*. New York: George H. Doran
Company, 1926. Print.

*Ladies and Gentlemen*. New York: Cosmopolitan Book Company, 1927.
Print.

*This Man's World*. London: Brentano, 1929. Print.

*Faith, Hope and Charity*. New York: Bobbs-Merrill, 1929. Print.

*One Way to Stop a Panic*. New York: Robert M. McBride, 1933.
Print.

*Azam: The Story of an Arabian Colt & His Friends*. Chicago: Rand
McNally, 1937. Print.

Cobb, Irvin S., et al. "Fishhead." New York: Barnes & Noble,
1993. Print.

**Travel**

*Some United States: A Series of Stops in Various Parts of this
Nation with one Excursion Across the Line*. New York:
George H. Doran, 1925. Print.

# Joseph Seamon Cotter, Sr.

## 1861-1949

Joseph Seamon Cotter's life spanned two centuries of monumental change for African Americans—the end of slavery in the 19th Century and the long battle for equality in the white-dominated world of the 20th Century. The great Black historian and author Joseph R. Kerlin said Joseph Seamon Cotter, Sr. was "... an Uncle Remus with culture and conscious art."

Cotter was a highly-regarded storyteller, poet, playwright, and educator who extoled the virtues of advancing his race. According to Joan R. Sherman in her work *Invisible Poets: Afro-Americans of the Nineteenth Century*, Cotter encouraged the self-help ethic, pride, humility, hard work, education, and a positive, optimistic outlook...

Cotter was born in Bardstown, Kentucky to Martha Vaughn, a literate and religious woman who was freeborn of mixed blood—half African, and half Native American and English. His father was Michael Cotter, a white man of Scotch-Irish ancestry. He learned to read by age four, but dropped out of school after completing the third grade to help support his family. He had no more formal education until 1883 when, at age twenty-two, he enrolled at a night school for African-American students in Louisville, Kentucky. Cotter attended this school for ten months, earning his high school diploma and teaching credentials.

He continued his education by studying at Indiana University, Kentucky State Industrial College, and Louisville Municipal College. There is no record of him having earned a college diploma, but by 1892 had earned life teaching certificates as a grammar teacher and school principal.

During a career in education that spanned over 50 years, he served in various teaching and administrative and capacities at Western Colored School, Ormsby Avenue Colored School, Eighth Street School, Paul Laurence Dunbar School, and Samuel Coleridge-Taylor School in the Louisville, Kentucky area. He founded the Paul Laurence Dunbar School in Louisville in 1893 and served as principal of this African-American high school until 1911. He then accepted an appointment as principal at Samuel Taylor Coleridge, a position he held until 1942. Paul Laurence Dunbar is said to have visited Cotter's family in 1894, which prompted several correspondence exchanges of poetry and discussions about the craft. Cotter maintained a lifetime friendship with him.

Cotter married fellow educator Maria F. Cox in 1891 and they had four children: Leonidas, Florence, Olivia, and Joseph Seamon Cotter Jr., who also became a promising poet but died at age twenty-three.

Cotter's early poems were published in prominent newspapers of the day, such as the *Louisville Courier Journal*. He won an Opportunity Prize Contest sponsored by the newspaper for his poem "The Tragedy of Pete." Cotter also contributed to various periodicals, including: *National Baptist Magazine, Voice of the Negro, Southern Teacher's Advocate*, and *Alexander's Magazine*.

Historian Joan R. Sherman says that during five decades of writing Cotter's interests ranged from industrial education in the 1890s to the "zoot suit." He was known to satirize the "the foibles and frailties" of African Americans. Cotter experimented with a variety of forms and styles of poetry; among those were the traditional ballad and various sonnet forms. His subject matter included social satire, historical tribute, racial issues, and philosophy.

Cotter died at his Louisville, Kentucky home on March 17, 1949 and is buried in the Greenwood Cemetery at Louisville.

### Sources

Cotter, Joseph Seamon, Sr. *Encyclopedia.com*. Online. Accessed 3 Dec. 2016.
<http://www.encyclopedia.com/education/news-wires-white-papers-and-books/cotter-joseph-seamon-sr-1861-1949#F>.

"Dr. Booker T. Washington to the National Negro Business League." *Poetry Foundation*. Online. Accessed 3 Dec. 2016.
<https://www.poetryfoundation.org/poems-and-poets/poems/detail/52440>.

"Frederick Douglass." *All Poetry*. Online. Accessed 3 Dec. 2016.
<https://allpoetry.com/poems/read_by/Joseph%20Seamon%2
0Coter%20%20%20%20Sr?page=1>.

"Joseph Seamon Cotter, Sr. (1861-1949)." *The Concise Oxford Companion to African American Literature*. Online. Accessed 3 Dec. 2016.
<http://www.oxfordreference.com/view/10.1093/oi/authority.20
110803095642167>.

"Joseph Seamon Cotter: A Poetic Pioneer." *African-American Registry*. Online. Accessed 4 Dec 2016.
<http://aaregistry.org/historic_events/view/joseph-seamon
cotter-poetic-pioneer>.

"Joseph S. Cotter." *Kentucky in American Letters Vol. II*. Ed. John Wilson Townsend. Cedar Rapids, IA: The Torch Press, 1913. 115-116. Print.

"Joseph Seamon Cotter." *The Kentucky Encyclopedia*. Ed. John Kleber. Lexington, KY: U P of Kentucky, 1992. 228-229. Print.

*"Joseph Seamon Cotter" Poetry.net* 3 Dec. 2016. Online. Accessed 5 Dec. 2015.
<http://www.poetry.net/poet/Joseph Seamon Cotter>.

"Joseph Seamon Cotter, Sr." *Poeticus*. Online. Accessed 5 Dec. 2016.
<https://www.poeticous.com/joseph-seamon-cotter?page=4>.

## Selected Bibliography

**Drama**

*Caleb, the Degenerate; A Play in Four Acts: A Study of the Types, Customs, and Needs of the American Negro.* Louisville, KY: Bradley & Gilbert Co., 1903. Print.

**Folktales**

*Negro Tales.* New York: Cosmopolitan Press, 1912. Print.

_____ (reprint). Santa Barbara, CA: Mnemosyne Press, 1969. Print.

**Poetry**

*A Rhyming.* Louisville, KY: New South Publishing, Co., 1895. Print.

\_\_\_\_\_ (reprint). Charleston, SC: Nabu Press, 2011. Print.

*Links of Friendship.* Louisville, KY: Bradley & Gilbert Co.,
      1898. Print.

*A White Song and a Black One.* Louisville, KY: Bradley &
      Gilbert Co., 1909. Print.

\_\_\_\_\_ (reprint). New York: AMS Press, 1975. Print.

\_\_\_\_\_ (reprint). Charleston, SC: Nabu Press, 2013. Print.

*Collected Poems.* New York: Henry Harrison, 1938. Print.

*Sequel to "The Pied Piper of Hamelin," and Other Poems.* New
      York: Henry Harrison, 1939. Print.

\_\_\_\_\_ (reprint). Santa Clarita, CA: Books for Libraries Press,
      1971. Print.

*Negroes and Others at Work and Play.* New York: Paebar Co.,
      1947. Print.

### Speeches

*Twenty-Fifth Anniversary of the Founding of Colored
      Parkland or "Little Africa" Louisville, Ky., 1801–1916.*
      Louisville, KY: I. Willis Cole Publishing Co., 1934. Print.

# A.B. Guthrie, Jr.

## 1901-1991

Bedford, Indiana native A.B. Guthrie, Jr. moved to Kentucky in 1926 to become a reporter with the *Lexington Leader* where he was to spend the next seventeen years as city editor, editorial writer, and executive editor. He began writing fiction in the early 1940s, publishing his first novel, *Murders at Moon Dance*, in 1943. In 1944, Harvard University awarded him a year-long Neiman Foundation Fellowship. The Fellowship allowed Guthrie to design an individual course of study in creative writing.

In 1947, he published *The Big Sky*, a sweeping epic novel tracing the 1830 journey of a group of frontiersmen from St. Louis to the Northwest Territory. Lewis Gannett, writing in *The New York*

*Herald Tribune,* called it a novel that "... belongs on the shelf beside the best stories Walter Edmonds and Kenneth Roberts have told of frontier days back East."

In 1947, Guthrie accepted a position as Professor of Creative Writing in the English Department at the University of Kentucky where he remained until 1952. This period was most productive for Guthrie, for it was during this time he wrote and published his 1949 novel *The Way West* which won the Pulitzer Prize for Fiction in 1950. This was another sweeping epic tale of a journey to the northwest, picking up where *The Big Sky* ended and telling the story of a group of men, women and children from Independence, Mo., travelling to the promised land of Oregon.

Actor Gary Cooper initially bought the film rights to *The Way West,* but never made the movie. He sold his rights for an estimated $40,000 to RKO/Winchester Productions. After some delay involving casting and production issues, Howard Hawks began filming in 1952. He cast Kirk Douglas, Dewey Martin, Arthur Hunnicutt, Jim Davis, and Elizabeth Threatt to fill the primary roles. Albeit a critical success, the film had lackluster box-office appeal. Another version of *The Way West,* directed by Andrew V. McLaglen, was released in 1967 and starred Kirk Douglas, Robert Mitchum, and Richard Widmark.

Guthrie was hired in 1951, by director George Stevens, to adapt Jack Schaefer's novel *Shane* to the movie screen. He received an Oscar nomination for his screenplay in 1953. In 1952, he was tagged by Hecht-Lancaster Productions to do the screen adaptation of Felix Holt's novel, *The Gabriel Horn,* which was given the movie title *The Kentuckian.*

Guthrie's reputation led 20th Century Fox to buy the rights to his 1957 novel, *These Thousand Hills,* before it was in final galleys. In 1958, the film was released and starred Richard Fleischer, Richard Egan, and Lee Remick. Guthrie published five additional novels in the 1960s and 1970s, but none received the acclaim that his work enjoyed through the 1940s and 1950s.

Guthrie's depicted an un-romanticized version of the settling of the West in America. Albeit, his fiction was replete with historical accuracy, his depictions of the challenges of the rugged landscape and frontier journeys were anything but idealized. Guthrie said of this practice: "I have a sense of morality about it. I want to talk about real people in real times. For every Wyatt Earp or Billy the Kid, there were thousands of people trying to get along."

His published works consisted of six novels, a book of essays, a children's book, a book of poems and five mystery novels.

Guthrie was married to Harriet Larson in 1931 and with her had two children, Alfred B. III, of Choteau, Montana and Helen Miller of Butte, Montana. After Harriet Guthrie died in the early 1960's, he married Carol B. Luthin (1969). She survived him, as did two stepchildren, Herbert Luthin, of Clarion, Pa., and Amy Sakariassen, of Bismarck, N.D. Guthrie died in 1991 and is buried on his ranch in Choteau, Montana.

## Sources

"A.B. Guthrie, Jr." *Kentucky in American Letters Volume III.*
    Georgetown, Kentucky: Georgetown U P, 1976. 139-141. Print.
Clark, Thomas D. "Alfred Bertram Guthrie, Jr." *The Kentucky*
    *Encyclopedia.* Ed. John Kleber. Lexington, KY: U P of Kentucky,
    1992. 395-396. Print.
Eder, Bruce. "A.B. Guthrie, Jr. Biography." *AllMovie.* Online.
    Accessed 29 Nov. 2016.
    <http://www.allmovie.com/artist/ab-guthrie-jr-p175743.>

Mowis, I.S. "A.B. Guthrie, Jr. Mini-Biography." *IMDB.com.*
Online. Accessed 29 Nov. 2016.
<http://www.imdb.com/name/nm0349238/bio>.

Severo, Richard. "A.B. Guthrie Jr Dead; Won Pulitzer for 'The
Way West.'" *New York Times* 27 April 1991. Online. Accessed
29 Nov. 2016.
<http://www.nytimes.com/1991/04/27/obituaries/ab-guthrie-jr-
is-dead-at-90-won-pulitzer-for-the-way-west.html>.

Stromme, Kari. "An Interesting Biography of A. B. Guthrie."
*The Bismarck Tribune.* 21 Jun 2009. Online. Accessed 7 Dec.
2016.
<http://bismarcktribune.com/news/local/an-interesting-biogra-
phy-of-a-b-guthrie/article_c23d81c2-b402-51fa-b0e9-0975553
a3c81.html>.

## Selected Bibliography

**Autobiography**
*Blue Hen's Chick: A Life in Context.* New York: McGraw-Hill,
1965. Print.

**Children's Books**
*Once Upon a Pond.* Missoula, MT: Mountain Press Publishing
Company, 1973. Print.

**Essays & Quotations**
*Images from the Great West.* LaCanada, CA: Chaco Press, 1990.
Print.

**History**
*Western Story: The Recollections of Charley O'Keiffe, 1844-1898.*
Omaha: U of Nebraska Press, 1960. Print.
*Doomed Road of Empire: The Spanish Trail of Conquest by Hodding
Carter.* New York: McGraw-Hill Book Company, 1963. Print.

**Novels**
*Murders at Moondance.* New York: E. P. Dutton & Co., 1943. Print.
*The Big Sky.* New York: William Sloane Associates, 1947. Print.
*The Way West.* New York: William Sloane Associates, 1949. Print.

*Trouble at Moondance*. New York: Popular Library, 1951. Print.

*These Thousand Hills*. Boston: Houghton-Mifflin Company, 1956.
Print.

*Arfive*. Boston: Houghton-Mifflin Company, 1971. Print.

*Wild Pitch*. Boston: Houghton-Mifflin Company, 1973. Print.

*The Last Valley*. Boston: Houghton-Mifflin Company, 1975. Print.

*The Genuine Article*. Boston: Houghton-Mifflin Company, 1977. Print.

*No Second Wind*. Boston: Houghton-Mifflin Company, 1980. Print.

*Fair Land, Fair Sky*. Boston: Houghton-Mifflin Company, 1982. Print.

*Playing Catch-Up*. Boston: Houghton-Mifflin Company, 1985. Print.

*Big Sky, Fair Land*. Flagstaff, AZ: Northland Press, 1988. Print.

**Poetry**

*Four Miles from Ear Mountain*. Missouli, MT: Kutenai Press, 1987. Print.

**Short Stories**

*The Big It and Other Stories*. Boston: Houghton-Mifflin Company,
1960. Print.

*Mountain Medicine*. New York: Cardinal Books, 1961. Print.

**Textbooks**

*A Field Guide to Writing Fiction*. Boston: Houghton-Mifflin Company,
1989. Print.

Photograph by Janet Worne Lexington Herald-Leader

# Gayl Jones

## 1949-

In a 1982 interview with Charles Rowell, Gayl Jones said that just like most people, she felt "... connections to home territory—connections that go into one's ideas of language, personality, landscape." Born to Franklin and Lucille Jones on November 23, 1949 in Lexington, Kentucky, Jones' early "connections" with the South are reflected strongly in her personal life as well as in her writing, which often brings Kentucky culture and characters to life for the reader.

Much of her desire to write came from her maternal grandmother, Amanda Wilson, who wrote plays for church productions, and from her mother, Lucille Jones, who wrote short stories to entertain Gayl and her brother Franklin, Jr. Jones says, "I have to say that if my mother hadn't written and read to me when I was growing up I probably wouldn't have even thought about it at all." In elementary school, several of Jones' instructors saw through her painfully shy exterior to the talented author blooming within and encouraged her to continue writing.

After graduating from Henry Clay High school, Jones took a considerable step away from her hometown and the South when she enrolled at Connecticut College. Her education there was funded through scholarships and support from the famed critic and fictionist Elizabeth Hardwick. In 1971, she received her Bachelor of Arts degree in English. She was then accepted into the graduate studies creative writing program at Brown University, where two years later she earned her Master of Arts degree in Creative Writing. By 1975, she had also earned her Doctorate of Arts degree in Creative Writing from Brown University. While at Brown, Jones had her first play, *Chile Woman*, produced.

Although she has written in genres such as poetry, short stories, and critical essays, Jones is best known for her novels. During her years at Brown, Jones studied under poet Michael Harper, who introduced her first novel *Corregidora* (1975) to Toni Morrison, who became her editor. Much of Jones' work explores a theme of contradictory and coexisting emotions. This theme, specifically of love and hate, is especially visible in *Corregidora*.

Following graduation, Jones' second novel, *Eva's Man* (1976), was published. She taught briefly at Wellesley College and then accepted a position as an assistant professor of English and Afro-American and African Studies at the University of Michigan.

During her tenure at the University of Michigan, Jones published a collection of short stories titled *White Rat* (1977), a volume-length poem *Songs for Anninho* (1981), and another volume of poetry titled *The Hermit-Woman* (1983). While at Michigan, Jones received fellowships from the National Endowment for the Arts and the Michigan Society of Fellows. She also met and married Robert Higgins, a politically active student, who eventually took her last name in marriage.

Because of legal problems, Jones and Higgins left the United States in the early 1980s and moved to Paris, France for a self-imposed five-year exile. During this time, Jones published another novel, *Die Volgelfaengerin/The Birdwatcher* (1984?) in Germany, as well as a collection of poetry, *Xarque and Other Poems* (1985), in the United States. Her first book of criticism, *Liberating Voices: Oral Tradition in African American Literature* (1991), was published soon after Jones and her husband returned to the United States in 1988. After living very privately in Lexington for ten years, Jones came again into the media spotlight for the release of a new novel, *The Healing* (1998), which became a finalist in the National Book Award competition. Her most recent novel *Mosquito* was published in 1999.

Jones often uses colloquial African-American dialect and stream-of-consciousness narration that fuses time and place throughout her novels. Jones commented on her use of this type of narration in an interview with Roseanne P. Bell in *Sturdy Black Bridges*:

> *One of the things I was consciously concerned with was the technique from the oral storytelling tradition that could be used in writing. A story is told to someone in much the same way when Ursa sings. She picks out someone to sing to. The book has layers of storytelling. Perceptions of time are important in the oral storytelling tradition in the*

*sense that you can make rapid transitions between
one period and the next, sort of direct transitions.*

Although Jones' work has often been contested because of her controversial subjects and persistent news coverage about her personal life, her work continues to awe readers with its complex style and depth of emotion. She draws many of the themes from her African-American heritage as well as her own personal life and struggles. Perhaps most important are the psychological depictions of her characters whose voices shout their story, their song, and their truth from the pages of her work. Her readers cannot wait to hear what will come next from this quiet woman who writes out loud.

### Sources

Tate, Claudia. *Black Women Writers at Work*. New York: Continuum, 1983. Print.

Chambers, Veronica. "The Invisible Woman Reappears—Sort of." *Newsweek*. CXXXI:7 (16 February 1998). 68. Print.

Clabough, Casey. "Toward feminine mythopoetic visions: the poetry of Gayl Jones." *African American Review* (22 March 2007). The Free Library. Online. Accessed 12 Jan. 2017. <https://www.thefreelibrary.com/African+American+Review/2007/March/22-p5121>.

*Corregidora*. New York: Random House, 1975. Print.

*Eva's Man*. New York: Random House, 1976. Print.

"Gayl Jones." *The Kentucky Anthology*. Ed. Wade Hall. Lexington, KY: The U P of Kentucky, 2005. 493-496. Print.

"Gayl Jones." *Voices from the Gaps: University of Minnesota*. Online. Accessed 12 Jan. 2017. <http://conservancy.umn.edu/bitstream/handle/11299/166239/jones,gayl.pdf?sequence=1>.

"Gayl Jones Essay: Critical Essays." *Enotes*. 131. Online. Accessed 12 Jan. 2017.
<https://www.enotes.com/topics/gayl-jones/critical-essays>.

*The Healing*. Boston: Beacon Press, 1998. Print.

Jordan, June. "All About Eva." *The New York Times Book Review* (16 May 1976). Online. Accessed 12 Jan. 2017.
<http://www.nytimes.com/1976/05/16/archives/all-about-eva-evas-man.html?_r=0>.

LaCroix, David. "Following her act: sequence and desire in Gayl Jones' *The Healing*." *African American Review* (22 March 2007). The Free Library. Online. Accessed 12 Jan. 2017.
<https://www.thefreelibrary.com/Following+her+act%3a+sequ ence+and+desire+in+Gayl+Jones%27s+The+Healing.- a0168334131>.

Riley, Carolyn & Phyllis Carmel Mendelson. *Contemporary Literary Criticism, Vol. 6*. Detroit, Michigan: Gale Research, 1976.

Rowell, Charles H. "An Interview with Gayl Jones." *Callaloo* 16.3 (1992). 32-53. Print.

*Sturdy Black Bridges*. Ed. Roseanne P. Bell, et al. New York: Anchor Press/Doubleday, 1979. 219+. Print.

## Selected Bibliography

**Academic**

Jones, Gayl. "Breaking out of the Conventions of Dialect: Dunbar and Hurston." *Presence Africaine: Revue Culturelle du Monde Noir* 144 (1987). Print.

Jones, Gayl. "Community and Voice: Gwendolyn Brooks' 'In the Mecca' A Life Distilled: Gwendolyn Brooks, Her Poetry and Fiction." *Presence Africaine: Revue Culturelle du Monde Noir* (1987). Print.

Jones, Gayl. "From The Quest from Wholeness: Re-Imagining the African-American Novel: An Essay on Third World Aesthetics." *Callaloo: A Journal of African-American and African Arts and Letters* (Summer 1994). Print.

## Collections

*Midnight Birds* (with Gayl Jones, Alice Walker, Toni Morrison, and
    Netozake Shange). Ed. Mary Helen Washington. New York:
    Anchor Books, 1980. Print.

*Black-eyed Susans and Midnight Birds: Stories by and About Black
    Women*(with Gayl Jones, et al). Ed. Mary Helen Washington
    New York: Anchor, 1989. Print.

*The Greywolf Annual Seven: Stories from the American Mosaic*
    (with Gayl Jones, et al). Saint Paul, MN: Greywolf Press,
    1990. Print.

## Folklore

*Liberating Voices: Oral Tradition in African American
    Literature*. Cambridge, MA.: Harvard U P, 1991. Print.

## Novels

*Corregidora*. New York: Random House, 1975. Print.

*Eva's Man*. New York: Random House, 1976. Print.

*Die Volgelfaengerin* (*The Birdwatcher*). Hamburger, Germany:
    RoRoRo (Rowohlt Verlag), 1984?. Print.

*The Healing*. Boston: Beacon Press, 1998. Print.

*The Healing, Corregidora, Eva's Man*. New York: Quality Paperback
    Book Club, 1998. Print.

*Mosquito*. Boston: Beacon Press, 1999. Print.

## Poetry

*Song for Anninho*. Detroit: Lotus Press, 1981. Print.

*The Hermit-Woman*. Detroit: Lotus Press, 1983. Print.

*Xarque & Other Poems*. Detroit: Lotus Press, 1985. Print.

*Song for Anninho*. Boston: Beacon Press, 1999. Print.

## Short Stories

*White Rat*. New York: Random House, 1977. Print.

_____ (reprint). New York: Harlem Moon Classics, 2005. Print.

Photograph by Annie Griffiths.

# Barbara Kingsolver

## 1955-

Matthew Gilbert of the *Boston Globe* characterized Barbara Kingsolver as the "... Woody Guthrie of contemporary American fiction...," primarily because social activism is at the core of most of her published work. What has driven Kingsolver throughout her writing career is a focus on environmental issues, political criticism and activism, and the role biological and scientific fact plays in interactions with the universe. She is concerned with the resulting consequences for citizens, families, and communities in their emerging world. Her ultimate focus has been on the relationship between art and politics, and man and nature.

Kingsolver was born on April 8, 1955 in Annapolis,

Maryland, the daughter of Dr. Wendell R. Kingsolver, a physician, and his wife, Virginia, but grew up in Carlisle, Kentucky in Nicholas County where her father had a medical practice. When she was seven, her father took the family to Léopoldville, Congo, where her parents worked as missionaries in public health. This experience later prompted Kingsolver to publish the novel *The Poisonwood Bible* (1998). This epic story about an Evangelical Christian family on a mission in Africa became her best known work. Selling over four million copies, this best seller was short-listed for both the Pulitzer Prize for Fiction and the Penn-Faulkner Award, won the National Book Prize of South Africa, and was an Oprah Winfrey "Oprah's Book Club" selection.

While researching for the novel, Kingsolver read Jonathan Kwitny's *Endless Enemies: The Making of an Unfriendly World* (1984), a book characterized as "America's worldwide war against its own best interests," and said of the experience: "The analogy struck me as novelesque: a study of this persistent human flaw— arrogance masquerading as help-fulness— could be a personal story that also functioned as allegory."

In addition to awards for *The Poisonwood Bible*, King-solver has been the recipient of numerous other awards and honors. Her most notable awards include: the 2000 National Humanities Medal (awarded by U.S. President Bill Clinton), James Beard Award, the Los Angeles Times Book Prize, the Edward Abbey EcoFiction Award, the Physicians for Social Responsibility National Award, and the Arizona Civil Liberties Union Award. Her novel *The Lacuna* won the 2010 Orange Prize for Fiction.

Every book that Kingsolver has written since her 1993

novel *Pigs in Heaven* has been on *The New York Times* Best Seller list. In 2011, she was awarded the Dayton Literary Peace Prize Richard C. Holbrooke Distinguished Achievement Award. Kingsolver is the first ever recipient of the newly named award to celebrate the U.S. diplomat who played an instrumental role in negotiating the Dayton Peace Accords in 1995. In 2014, she was awarded the Lifetime Achievement Award by the Library of Virginia. The award recognizes outstanding and long-lasting contributions to literature by a Virginian. Additionally, Kingsolver was named one the most important writers of the 20th Century by *Writers Digest*.

Kingsolver holds a B.A. in Biology from DePauw University (magna cum laude) and a M.S. in Biology and Ecology from the University of Arizona. She has held a variety of jobs including: archeologist, art class model, grant writer, housecleaner, X-ray technician, biological research assistant, medical document translator, copy editor, typesetter, science writer, and feature writer for journals and newspapers. Since 1985, she has focused on writing and publishing, having published numerous freelance newspaper and magazine articles and 14 books including novels, short stories, and essays.

In a 2010 interview, she discussed her fiction with Maya Jaggi of *The Guardian*:

> *I don't understand how any good art could fail to be political. Good fiction creates empathy. A novel takes you somewhere and asks you to look through the eyes of another person... the creation of empathy necessarily influences how you'll behave to other people. It is... a powerful craft...*

Kingsolver has plied this power to create indelible characters and stories that draw the reader into their saga and circumstances.

One seminal moment, in the direction of Kingsolver's thematic focus, came when she moved with her first husband, Joe Hoffmann, to a small cabin in the desert outside Tucson, Arizona; where they became active in organizations investigating human-rights violations and supporting Latin American refugees seeking asylum. She later wrote of the experience:

> I had come to the Southwest expecting cactus, wide open spaces, and adventure. I found, instead, another whole America... this desert that burned with raw beauty had a great fence built across it, attempting to divide north from south. I'd stumbled upon a borderland where people perished of heat by day and cold hostility by night.

This set the course for her activism, not only in human rights, but in other political issues. Since then, Kingsolver has been deeply involved with disparate parts of America.

Barbara Kingsolver says of her writing process: "I tend to wake up very early. Too early... I always wake with sentences pouring into my head. So getting to my desk every day feels like a long emergency. It's a funny thing: people often ask how I discipline myself to write. I can't begin to understand the question. For me, the discipline is turning off the computer and leaving my desk to do something else."

## Sources

"Barbara Kingsolver." *The Kentucky Anthology*. Ed. Wade Hall. Lexington: The U P of Kentucky, 2005. 532. Print.

"Barbara Kingsolver Biography." *Biography.Com*. Online. Accessed 21 Nov. 2016.
<http://www.biography.com/people/barbara-kingsolver-20836751>.

"Barbara Kingsolver Biography." *Encyclopedia of World Biography*. Online. Accessed 22 November 2016.
<http://www.notablebiographies.com/newsmakers2/2005-Fo-La/Kingsolver-Barbara.html>.

"Barbara Kingsolver on the Poisonwood Bible—Guardian Book Club." *theguardian*. 11 May 2013. Online. Accessed 21 Nov. 2016.
<https://www.theguardian.com/books/2013/may/11/book-club-barbara-kingsolver-poisonwood>.

"Barbara Kingsolver Reveals Herself." *Barbara Kingsolver: The Authorized Site*. Online. Accessed 23 Nov. 2016.
<http://www.kingsolver.com/biography/autobiography.html>.

Charney, Noah. "Barbara Kingsolver: How I Write." *The Daily Beast* 5 Dec. 2012. Online. Accessed 21 Nov. 2016.
<http://www.thedailybeast.com/articles/2012/12/05/barbara-kingsolver-how-i-write.html>.

Hall, Wade. "Barbara Kingsolver." *The Kentucky Encyclopedia*. Ed. John E. Kleber. Lexington, KY: The U P of Kentucky, 1992. 519. Print.

Jaggi, Maya. "A Life in Writing: Barbara Kingsolver." *theguardian* 11 June 2010. Online. Accessed 21 Nov. 2016.
<https://www.theguardian.com/books/2010/jun/12/life-in-writing-barbara-kingsolver>.

## Selected Bibliography

### Essays

*High Tide in Tucson: Essays from Now or Never*. New York: HarperCollins, 1995. Print.

*Small Wonder*. New York: Harper Collins, 2002. Print.

*Last Stand: America's Virgin Lands* (photographs by Annie Griffiths
 Belt). Washington: National Geographic Society, 2002. Print.

**Non-Fiction**

*Animal, Vegetable, Miracle: A Year of Food Life*. New York:
 HarperCollins, 2007. Print.

**Novels**

*The Bean Trees*. New York: Harper & Row, 1988. Print.

*Animal Dreams*. New York: Harper Perennial, 1990. Print.

*Pigs in Heaven*. New York: Harper Perennial, 1993. Print.

*The Poisonwood Bible*. New York: HarperCollins, 1998. Print.

*Prodigal Summer*. New York: HarperCollins, 2000. Print.

*The Lacuna*. New York: HarperCollins, 2009. Print.

*Flight Behavior*. New York: HarperCollins, 2012. Print.

**History**

*Holding the Line: Women in the Great Arizona Mine Strike of
 1983*. Ithaca, NY: Cornell U P, 1989. Print.

**Poetry**

*Another America/Otra América*. Seattle, WA: Seal Press, 1992. Print.

**Short Fiction**

*Homeland and Other Stories*. New York: Harper & Row, 1989. Print.

# About the Author:
# James B. Goode

Professor, poet, fictionist, filmmaker, and photographer James B. Goode is Professor Emeritus of English on the faculty of Bluegrass Community & Technical College in Lexington, Kentucky. Goode holds undergraduate and graduate degrees from the University of Kentucky and a MFA in Creative Writing: Fiction from Murray State University. He has been a visiting Professor of English at The University of Wales at Swansea, Changsha University in Hunan, China, and Maseno University in Kenya, Africa. He currently serves as Coordinator of the Kentucky Writers Hall of Fame at the Carnegie Center in Lexington, Kentucky. Additionally, he is a mentor in the Carnegie Center's Authors Academy. He is an award-winning author of six books and has published numerous poems, short stories, and essays in magazines such as *South Carolina Review, Huron Review, Ball State University Forum, The Journal of Appalachian Studies, Appalachian Heritage, Journal of Kentucky Studies, Pluck: The Journal of Affrilachian Arts & Culture*, and *Kentucky Monthly*. His most recent book *Kentucky's Twelve Days of Christmas* is an anthology of fiction, creative non-fiction, poetry, and songs by prominent Kentucky writers.

James B. Goode in Paris, France. *(Photograph by Candace Hale)*

CPSIA information can be obtained
at www.ICGtesting.com
Printed in the USA
LVOW08*0855240617
538920LV00004BB/10/P